Quotes to raise children by or At least survive raising them!

Voldane Pelt & Matthew Stout

Voldane Pelt and Matthew Stout have asserted their moral right to be identified as the authors of this book in accordance with the ***Copyright Designs and Patents Act of 1988.***

Copyright © 2019 Be Better Publishing

All rights reserved.

ISBN: 978-1-7329797-5-8

Table of Contents

Quotes to raise children by or At least survive raising them! i

Introduction vi

Time is Precious 1

    Time is Precious 1

Sit, Stay Roll Over Discipline 22

School Day Blues 39

Eat Your Veggies. Food. 69

Life with kiddos 98

Dating & Kids 117

The Birds & the Bees - Safe Sex? Uh... here read this. 135

Toddlers 160

Teenagers 196

Pulling Hair, At the end of the Rope, Inspirational 221

Sports & Music 277

Pregnancy, because it all begins, with a big belly 310

Quotes for Parents

Introduction

Memory is fragile, sometimes we feel alone and once in a while our kids say the damndest things and we want to record them. This quote book has a companion workbook, so you never lose a moment & always have someone to vent to.

Parents need advice & often a quote is all they have time for. This book will make you smile, inspire you —and hopefully remind you that you're not alone. —

You're a parent and that means you are dealing with the most rewarding, exhausting and frightening job in the universe. They have millions and millions of books about how to raise a kid what to do, say and how.

Do you ever wonder how parents have time to read all those pages of instructions? Or if you have read some of them do you have a sneaking suspicion the kids, they were written for were not from the same species as yours?

As parents, you have a well of instinct that is the only instruction manual you need. It just gets plugged up with hair and grease, like a drain, bubble gum; and this fascination with looking under, through or walking into bathrooms while you're trying to ahem well you know.

Quotes have this power to inspire, unclog the drain of your parenting instincts and get the gum holding you back as a parent out of the way. The quotes and thoughts here are not meant to tell you how, why or when to be a parent. That would be silly your raising unique individual little people with unique situations.

What these quotes are intended to do is help you find your smile and reconnect you with those little moments of understanding how to be a great parent to your special little person. Go ahead put this in your purse beside the kitchen sink and car keys. When you feel down or overwhelmed read a few quotes and see if you can find that well of parenting instinct again.

I guarantee it's still there, sometimes it just needs to be unclogged like the toilet.

"Why is your sister's Barbie stuck in the toilet George?"

"She's mean! She wouldn't go out with my Gi Joe!"

"And the roll of toilet paper in there with her?"

Giggles, "She's upside down and has no pants on. You're not supposed to see, you know."

Quotes for Parents

Time is Precious

Time is endless and vast so why aren't we drowning in it? Remember how time used to always be there when you needed it? Now as parents its emptier than the bank account and a big cowl wearing guy with a sickle is looking to close your account if we don't get some more time deposited.

These quotes all have to do with finding, losing and time in general. Take a breath soccer practice and piano lessons will still be there after you read a few. In the meantime, I will be writing a letter to that cowled guy with the big sickle about an extension on my own time account.

I hope he can read...

—

Time is Precious

Oh, how time flies. They are so small, fragile and precious one day and obnoxious teenagers the next. You blink and they are amazing young adults. Then before you turn around, you're a grandparent.

Sometimes in our modern plastic and materialistic world children and parents get hypnotized by shiny things that make noise and on television, they seem to offer the answers to happiness. Yet at the end of the day, all we have are the experiences and shared memories to connect us with each other, especially our children.

Time the most precious and rare gift we have to give as it is all that is ever fully ours. I hope this chapter helps you fight the shiny object syndrome so many suffer from today.

Not every quote here will say children in it. Some will be speaking of time and how we choose to use it, period. But just like all wisdom think of children as you read the quote and I believe you will understand why the quote was included here.

Voldane Pelt

HEIGH HO!—time creeps but slow;
  I've looked up the hill so long;
None come this way, the sun sinks low,
  And my shadow's very long.

They said I should sail in a little boat,
  Up the stream, by the great white mill;
But I've waited all day, and none come my way;
  I've waited—I'm waiting still.

They said I should see a fairy town,
  With houses all of gold,
And silver people, and a gold church steeple;—
  But it wasn't the truth they told.

Voldane Pelt

"Children spell love TIME." Many people have said this in many ways, and it is true.

—

M. Grundler

"The best inheritance a parent can give to his children is a few minutes of their time each day."

—

Jesse Jackson

"Your children need your presence more than your presents."

—

Barbara Bush

"At the end of your life, you will never regret not having passed one more test, not winning one more verdict, or not closing one more deal. You will regret time not spent with a husband, a friend, a child, a parent."

—

Michael J. Fox

"Family is not an important thing. It's everything."

—

Reba McEntire

"I don't think quantity time is as special as quality time with your family."

—

Jim Rohn

"Your family and your love must be cultivated like a garden. Time, effort, and imagination must be summoned constantly to keep any relationship flourishing and growing."

—

Dave Willis

"If you are too busy to enjoy time with your family, then you need to reevaluate your priorities."

—

Boyd K. Packer

"Family time is sacred time and should be protected and respected."

—

Abigail Van Buren

"If you want your children to turn out well, spend twice as much time with them and half as much money."

—

Jennifer Ellison

"Going home and spending time with your family and your real friends keeps you grounded."

—

Walt Disney

"A man should never neglect his family for business."

—

Marlon Brando

"Do you spend time with your family? Good. Because a man that doesn't spend time with his family can never be a real man."

—

Claire Shipman

"Valuing time with your family does not mean you've lost your ambition. Define success for yourself."

—

Matthew Quick

"You need to make time for your family no matter what happens in your life."

—

Brandy Norwood

"Your children can be around you all day, but if you don't spend quality time with them and you don't pay attention to them and talk to them and listen to them, it doesn't matter that they're just around you."

—

Voldane Pelt

This one made me stop and realize that this is also how we should count our time spent with our children, not in minutes or hours.

—

Aristotle

"We live in deeds, not years; in thoughts, not breaths; In feelings, not in figures on a dial. We should count time by heartthrobs. He most lives who thinks most, feels the noblest, acts the best."

—

Earl Nightingale

"Learn to enjoy every minute of your life. Be happy now. Don't wait for something outside of yourself to make you happy in the future. Think how really precious the time is you have to spend, whether it's at work or with your family. Every minute should be enjoyed and savored."

—

Voldane Pelt

This next one had me wondering how long I could play chase with kids and then I thought what about my grandkids or catch a ball. Even going for a walk with them where everything is new and exciting again because I am with them is limited by time.

—

Viggo Mortensen

"Life is short and the older you get, the more you feel it. Indeed, the shorter it is. People lose their capacity to walk, run, travel, think, and experience life. I realize how important it is to use the time I have."

—

Voldane Pelt

So often I will hear people brag about how many jobs or hours they work to give their kids what they didn't have. I want to print this and place it on their front door so before they leave, they can at least reconsider their priorities.

—

Jim Rohn

"Time is more value, than money. You can get more money, but you cannot get more time."

—

Voldane Pelt

This happens so often with kids they even wrote a song about it. We talk about taking our kids and doing things all the time but somehow, we often talk more than doing.

—

Bruce Lee

"If you spend too much time thinking about a thing, you'll never get it done."

—

John C. Maxwell

"Time management is an oxymoron. Time is beyond our control, and the clock keeps ticking regardless of how we lead our lives. Priority management is the answer to maximizing the time we have."

Voldane Pelt

How often as parents do, we or are we tempted to lecture children on not wasting time? This one bears some reflection before we continue doing that.

—

John Lennon

"Time you enjoy wasting was not wasted."

—

Voldane Pelt

Whatever your beliefs these words should guide how we spend every moment. Too often we rent our today to pay for something tomorrow.

—

Mother Teresa

"Yesterday is gone. Tomorrow has not yet come. We have only today. Let us begin."

Voldane Pelt

Kids are smart they understand this often better than we do.

Lao Tzu

"Time is a created thing. To say, 'I don't have time' is like saying, 'I don't want to.'"

Voldane Pelt

They are always watching and listening taking it all in. That is terrifying when you think about it because when we're not speaking to them, they are learning the most.

Clarence Budington Kelland

"My father didn't tell me how to live; he lived and let me watch him do it."

Dave Pelzer

"Childhood should be carefree, playing in the sun; not living a nightmare in the darkness of the soul."

—

Voldane Pelt

This next one may seem out of place in a chapter about time but think of how rare it is today for so many children to be in nature. Not just looking out the window or from the groomed landscaped park with its gravel and cold metal swings but immersed in it as we are meant to be. Most of us adults would benefit from time spent in it as well.

—

Pat Conroy

"To describe our growing up in the low country of South Carolina, I would have to take you to the marsh on a spring day, flush the great blue heron from its silent occupation, scatter marsh hens as we sink to our knees in mud, open an oyster with a pocketknife and feed it to you from the shell and say, 'There. That taste. That's the taste of my childhood'."

—

Orson Scott Card

"Being young is an 18-year prison sentence for a crime your parents committed. But you do get time off for good behavior."

—

Voldane Pelt

We took a vacation once every few years usually with extended family. But it was the travels I shared with my mom as she read to me that I treasured the most.

—

Orson Scott Card

"If you read to your kids, you'll make readers out of them, partly because they'll associate reading with good parent time."

Voldane Pelt

I included this one because so many of the quotes about children, family and time can be misleading. The entire family together doing things is wonderful. But there will always be things that one parent or the other, one child or another prefer doing and pairing of that way is natural, healthy and important.

—

Patricia Wright

"Lemurs are good parents, but they do it in different ways. I originally studied father care. I was very interested in that and we saw that a lot of these animals that lived in pairs and the father wasn't doing anything at all for the first month. But then suddenly, when the baby got to be a certain weight then the dads chipped in and started carrying the babies which was very nice. And then if there was twins or triplets then they helped."

—

Dwayne Johnson

"The challenges that I face today are the same challenges we all face. Trying to balance your life between work, family, loved ones, your husband, your wife - boyfriend or girlfriend. If you have kids - balancing that, balancing your work with the time you spend with your kids. The idea of wanting to be a good parent and then the motivation to be a great parent. Whether you're black, white, any color. Rich, poor, regardless of religion, cousins of culture, we go through those. We have the same challenges."

—

Voldane Pelt

This next one is about education but also the couch and how much time we as parents as well as our kids spend on it. I often think a home without a couch and television would be more of a home.

—

Arnold Schwarzenegger

"I take the academic education as seriously as the physical education. That's why I tell parents that the schools can't do it all themselves. The parents can't come home from work and turn on the TV. That's not being a good parent."

"OUR CHILDREN ARE COUNTING ON US TO PROVIDE TWO THINGS: CONSISTENCY AND STRUCTURE. CHILDREN NEED PARENTS WHO SAY WHAT THEY MEAN, MEAN WHAT THEY SAY, AND DO WHAT THEY SAY THEY ARE GOING TO DO."

BARBARA COLOROSO

Urie Bronfenbrenner

"In order to develop normally, a child requires progressively more complex joint activity with one or more adults who have an irrational emotional relationship with the child. Somebody's got to be crazy about that kid. That's number one. First, last and always."

Jean Liedloff

It is our genetic nature as a species to believe as young children that our parents and elders are right. We watch them to see what's what. Later on we can judge for ourselves and rebel if need be, but when we're just months old, or a year or two, and a parent looks at us with impatience, or disgust, or disdain, or just leaves us there to cry and doesn't answer us even though we're longing to be embraced and nurtured, we assume that something must be wrong with us. Unfortunately, at that age, it's impossible to think there might be something wrong with them.

Thomas S. Monson

"Raising children, be aware that the piles and piles of laundry will disappear all too soon and that you will, to your surprise, miss them profoundly."

—

M. Scott Peck

"The time and the quality of the time that their parents devote to them indicate to children the degree to which they are valued by their parents. ... When children know that they are valued, when they truly feel valued in the deepest parts of themselves, then they feel valuable. This knowledge is worth more than any gold."

—

CHILDREN NEED TO LEARN TO TAKE RESPONSIBILITY FOR THEIR ACTIONS SO THAT THEY DO NOT BECOME ADULTS BELIEVING THAT NOTHING IS EVER THEIR FAULT.

Sit, Stay Roll Over Discipline

This chapter we look at one of the most frequent parts of parenting, discipline or the lack thereof. With a subject as controversial as this one often is please remember these quotes are to make you smile and maybe think for a little while.

You will not agree with all of these and should not. But even those you disagree and disapproves of rather the quoted or the quote itself add a little salt.

Smile and indulge this little while in some quotes starting with a few scenes from yesteryear.

Voldane Pelt

Engaged in a Disgraceful Fight.

FEW scenes are more painful than a street fight between lads of tender years, who, unrestrained by proper training, give vent to their passions. In after-years the quarrelsome boy is likely to become a harsh and cruel man, unfitted for good society or companionship.

Children that Know How to be Happy.

QUIET groves, green grass and summer air, where happy little children sport innocently amid the beauties of nature, speaking kind words and engaging harmoniously in their plays, shadow forth the peaceful dispositions and pursuits of their future lives.

Getting into Bad Company.

NO matter how good a boy is, if he falls into the society of vicious lads, and suffers himself to listen to their vile language and wicked schemes, he soon loses his innocence, gradually sinks into immoral habits, and becomes a *criminal*.

Good Society Brings Prosperity.

BY associating only with the pure and good, an innocent boy will save himself from falling into many hurtful snares, and in such society he will find healthful restraint and great encouragement, which will better prepare him for a prosperous manhood.

Maya Angelou

"There are great parents of small children - they keep their little hair in bows - but those parents are not always good parents of young adults. As soon as their children get up to some size, it's "Shut up, sit down, you talk too much, keep your distance, I'll send you to Europe!" My mom was a terrible parent of small children but a great parent of young adults. She'd talk to me as if I had some sense."

—

Lucile Hadžihalilović

"I had good parents. Nothing terrible happened. But I had the feeling that they kind of protected me from reality somehow."

—

Anthony Edwards

"It's difficult to keep that perspective, I think, as a parent: to know your boundaries as to what's good parenting or just projecting your own expectations on your kids. That's the hardest."

—

Parker J. Palmer

"Every good teacher and every good parent has somehow learned to negotiate the paradox of freedom and discipline. We want our children and our students to become people who think and live freely, yet at the same time, we know that helping them become free requires us to restrict their freedom in certain situations."

—

Voldane Pelt

While I understand this next one is dead on as far as our society views things for me it highlights why society has no business raising children. I don't want tame children who will become tame sheeple and follow without question or conscience. I want bright-eyed, curios and demanding children that require a parent to actively listen, speak and be alive to match their enthusiasm for life.

—

Frank Zappa

"The more boring a child is, the more the parents, when showing off the child, receive adulation for being good parents — because they have a tame child-creature in their house."

—

Voldane Pelt

I must not be a good parent because I would not be okay with being hated by my child. But then my definition of hate and love is often deeper than most peoples.

—

Alain de Botton

"The good parent: someone who doesn't mind, for a time, being hated by their children."

—

Gary Smalley

"Affirming words from moms and dads are like light switches. Speak a word of affirmation at the right moment in a child's life and it's like lighting up a whole roomful of possibilities."

—

William Martin

"You do not have to make your children into wonderful people. You just have to remind them that they are wonderful people. If you do this consistently from the day, they are born they will believe it easily."

—

Anne Lamott

"One thing I know for sure about raising children is that every single day a kid needs discipline... But also, every single day a kid needs a break."

—

Sadie Frost

"I was a very defiant child, and my father encouraged that. He wanted me to be as wild and creative as possible and didn't believe in disciplining children."

—

Ricardo Montalban

"There couldn't be better parents than mine, loving yet strict. They disciplined with love. A child without discipline is, in a way, a lost child. You cannot have freedom without discipline."

It is not what you do for your children, but what you have taught them to do for themselves, that will make them successful human beings.

Ann Landers

Gordon Neufeld

"Many people think that discipline is the essence of parenting. But that isn't parenting. Parenting is not telling your child what to do when he or she misbehaves. Parenting is providing the conditions in which a child can realize his or her full human potential."

—

Amy Chua

"I see my upbringing as a great success story. By disciplining me, my parents inculcated self-discipline. And by restricting my choices as a child, they gave me so many choices in my life as an adult. Because of what they did then, I get to do the work I love now."

—

Voldane Pelt

This is something public schools must be taught.

—

James E. Faust

"One of the most difficult parental challenges is to appropriately discipline children. Child-rearing is so individualistic. Every child is different and unique. What works with one may not work with another."

—

Danny Silk

"The difference between punishment and discipline is a powerful child."

—

Bette Davis

"Discipline is a symbol of caring to a child. He needs guidance. If there is love, there is no such thing as being too tough with a child."

—

Maria Montessori

"The undisciplined child enters into discipline by working in the company of others; not being told he is naughty." "Discipline is, therefore, primarily a learning experience and less a punitive experience if appropriately dealt with."

—

Maria Montessori

"At a given moment a child becomes interested in a piece of work, showing it by the expression of his face, by his intense attention, by his perseverance in the same exercise. That child has set foot upon the road leading to discipline."

—

Maria Montessori

"Discipline must come through liberty. . ... We do not consider an individual disciplined only when he has been rendered as artificially silent as a mute and as immovable as a paralytic. He is an individual annihilated, not disciplined."

—

Simon Baron-Cohen

"Parents who discipline their child by discussing the consequences of their actions produce children who have better moral development, compared to children whose parents use authoritarian methods and punishment."

—

John Bradshaw

"Children need parents who model self-discipline rather than preach it. They learn from what their parents are willing to do; not from what they say they do."

—

Marva Collins

"An error means a child needs help, not a reprimand or ridicule for doing something wrong."

—

Jackie Chan

"The children right now, the young children, everybody should go to a martial arts school. Why? Because as soon as they go to a martial arts school, they learn discipline."

—

Robert Orben

"Never raise your hand to your children - it leaves your midsection unprotected."

—

Bill Ayers

"Your kids require you most of all to love them for who they are, not to spend your whole time trying to correct them."

—

Diana Loomans

"If I had my child to raise all over again, I'd finger paint more, and point the fingerless. I'd do less correcting, and more connecting. I'd take my eyes off my watch, and watch with my eyes. I would care to know less, and know to care more. I'd take more hikes and fly more kites. I'd stop playing serious, and seriously play. I'd run through more fields, and gaze at more stars. I'd do more hugging, and less tugging. I would be firm less often and affirm much more. I'd build self-esteem first, and the house later. I'd teach less about the love of power, and more about the power of love."

—

School Day Blues

Today more than ever before we as parents must be actively involved in our children's education. Public, private or homeschooling all is predicated on the parent knowing what their child is being taught. If parents do not call out corrupt politicians slipping in controversial propaganda, inaccurate history or simply not being up to the parent's standards no one will.

This chapter is all about that amazing time when a child begins learning to read, add and subtract and develop their own interests. It is sad, amazing and can be incredibly rewarding. I hope these quotes help you remember this time for the amazing opportunity it is even as it can be a sad time as well.

Many of these have to do with the ongoing dilemma of improving the public school for all children. As I mentioned before I strongly believe that the largest hurdle in public school success for children is to stop the fiction that a one size fits all approach is sane.

While you may find some of these redundant simply pass over them and go on to quotes that you find more inspiring and thought-provoking. Once again you should not agree with all of these as many are contradictory and all should make you think, smile or both.

Voldane Pelt

Quotes for Parents

David Elkind

"Infants and young children are not just sitting twiddling their thumbs, waiting for their parents to teach them to read and do math. They are expending a vast amount of time and effort in exploring and understanding their immediate world. Healthy education supports and encourages this spontaneous learning."

—

Mem Fox

"The fire of literacy is created by the emotional sparks between a child, a book, and the person reading. It isn't achieved by the book alone, nor by the child alone, nor by the adult who's reading aloud—it's the relationship winding between all three, bringing them together in easy harmony."

—

Maya Angelou

"The best candy shop a child can be left alone in is the library"

—

Voldane Pelt

With the import placed on tests and stale memorization of numbers and dates that so often is overwhelming in school this next quote should be remembered by parents or we may be better educators on the things that really matter.

—

Matt Damon

"I think what's important for kids to know is that your decisions here on earth matter, your behavior matters and how you treat other people matters."

—

Jacque Fresco

"If you had a free society you couldn't get people to go to war if you had an intelligent type of upbringing in one's children. They would say; There must be many other ways of solving problems other than killing people."

—

Dalai Lama

"Modern education is premised strongly on materialistic values. It is vital that when educating our children's brains that we do not neglect to educate their hearts, a key element of which has to be the nurturing of our compassionate nature."

—

Jacque Fresco

"We are not taught to be thinkers, but reflectors of our culture. Let's teach our children to be thinkers."

—

Voldane Pelt

This quote is a prime example of the critical education to often neglected in the modern world. An adult can learn to read or add but an adult that never learned to love will always struggle with understanding love. In public school, we teach children that they must wait to use the bathroom even if it's an emergency, to get in line, to be silent, to obey first, and then thinking & caring is lost.

—

Alice Miller

"Children who are respected learn respect. Children who are cared for learn to care for those weaker than themselves. Children who are loved for what they are cannot learn intolerance. In an environment such as this, they will develop their own ideals, which can be nothing other than humane, since they grew out of the experience of love."

—

Rudolf Dreikurs

"We cannot protect our children from life. Therefore, it is essential that we prepare them for it."

—

Voldane Pelt

Often, we must remind the school system of this, and if that doesn't work, we must insist on it.

—

Florence Littauer

"Our children do not need a makeover; they just need to be understood. If you understand their emotional needs now, you can save them a lifetime of searching for what they never had as a child."

—

Rudolf Dreikurs

"A child needs encouragement like a plant needs water."

—

Dr. Seuss

"A person's a person, no matter how small."

—

Maria Montessori

"The task of the educator lies in seeing that the child does not confound good with immobility, and evil with activity, as often happens in old-time discipline . . . A room in which all the children move about usefully, intelligently, and voluntarily, without committing any rough or rude act, would seem to me, a classroom very well disciplined indeed."

Angela Davis

"When children attend schools that place a greater value on discipline and security than on knowledge and intellectual development, they are attending prep schools for prison."

John Taylor Gatto

"Children do not learn in school; they are babysat. It takes maybe 50 hours to teach reading, writing, and arithmetic. After that, students can teach themselves. Mainly what school does is to keep the children off the streets and out of the job market."

John Taylor Gatto

"It is absurd and anti-life to be part of a system that compels you to listen to a stranger reading poetry when you want to learn to construct buildings or to sit with a stranger discussing the construction of buildings when you want to read poetry."

Voldane Pelt

I am sure many will say of course we need public school. They will speak of social interaction and all the other justifications. The reason I put this here is so you can think for a minute. Is public school what real life is like? And if not, why would you want your child learning social interaction in a dictatorship where they can't even decide for themselves when they have to go to the bathroom. If we need public school, we need to take back control of it from the government and return it to the people.

John Taylor Gatto

"Do we really need school? I don't mean education, just forced schooling: six classes a day, five days a week, nine months a year, for twelve years. Is this deadly routine really necessary? And if so, for what? Don't hide behind reading, writing, and arithmetic as a rationale, because 2 million happy homeschoolers have surely put that banal justification to rest."

Malcolm X

"Education is an important element in the struggle for human rights. It is the means to help our children and thereby increase self-respect. Education is our passport to the future, for tomorrow belongs to the people who prepare for it today."

Voldane Pelt

This next one made me wonder if the public school has gotten better in this regard since, he said this, and I came to the conclusion that it has not. Judge for yourself not just based on who said this but from every ethnicity, culture, and heritage in the world. Perhaps it is up to us as parents to provide books from the library to share more cultures and heritages because there are so many around the world that one child would need a hundred lifetimes to scratch the surface.

Malcolm X

"When we send our children to school, they learn nothing about us other than we used to be cotton pickers. Why your grandfather was Nat Turner; your grandfather was Toussaint L'Ouverture; your grandfather was Hannibal. It was your grandfather's hands who forged civilization and it was your grandmother's hands who rocked the cradle of civilization. But the textbooks tell our children nothing."

—

Maria Montessori

"The education of even a small child, therefore, does not aim at preparing him for school, but for life."

—

Maria Montessori

"How can we speak of Democracy or Freedom when from the very beginning of life, we mould the child to undergo tyranny, to obey a dictator? How can we expect democracy when we have reared slaves? Real freedom begins at the beginning of life, not at the adult stage. These people who have been diminished in their powers, made short-sighted, devitalized by mental fatigue, whose bodies have become distorted, whose wills have been broken by elders who say: "your will must disappear and mine prevail!"-how can we expect them, when school-life is finished, to accept and use the rights of freedom?"

—

Maria Montessori

"To consider the school as a place where instruction is given is one point of view. But, to consider the school as a preparation for life is another. In the latter case, the school must satisfy all the needs of life."

—

Maria Montessori

"We cannot know the consequences of suppressing a child's spontaneity when he is just beginning to be active. We may even suffocate life itself. That humanity which is revealed in all its intellectual splendor during the sweet and tender age of childhood should be respected with a kind of religious veneration. It is like the sun which appears at dawn or a flower just beginning to bloom. Education cannot be effective unless it helps a child to open up himself to life."

—

John Dewey

"How can the child learn to be a free and responsible citizen when the teacher is bound?"

—

George Bernard Shaw

"What we want is to see the child in pursuit of knowledge, and not knowledge in pursuit of the child."

—

George Bernard Shaw

"The only time my education was interrupted was when I was in school."

—

George Bernard Shaw

"My schooling not only failed to teach me what it professed to be teaching but prevented me from being educated to an extent which infuriates me when I think of all I might have learned at home by myself."

—

George Bernard Shaw

"There is, on the whole, nothing on earth intended for innocent people so horrible as a school. To begin with, it is a prison. But in some respects, more cruel than a prison. In a prison, for instance, you are not forced to read books written by the warders and the governor. . . .In the prison, you are not forced to sit listening to turnkeys discoursing without charm or interest on subjects that they don't understand and don't care about, and therefore incapable of making you understand or care about. In a prison, they may torture your body, but they do not torture your brains."

—

George Bernard Shaw

"As people get their opinions so largely from the newspapers they read, the corruption of the schools would not matter so much if the Press were free. But the Press is not free. As it costs at least a quarter of a million of money to establish a daily newspaper in London, the newspapers are owned by rich men. And they depend on the advertisements of other rich men. Editors and journalists who express opinions in print that are opposed to the interests of the rich are dismissed and replaced by subservient ones."

—

George Bernard Shaw

"The practical question, then, is what to do with the children. Tolerate them at home we will not. Let them run loose in the streets we dare not until our streets become safe places for children, which, to our utter shame, they are not at present, though they can hardly be worse than some homes and some schools.

—

Jamie Oliver

"Every child should be taught to cook in school, not just talk about nutrition all day. Good food can be made in 15 minutes. This could be the first generation where the kids teach the parents."

—

Marian Wright Edelman

"We're spending, on average, three times more for prison than for public-school pupils. That's the dumbest investment policy. It doesn't make us safer."

—

Bill Gates

"If you think your teacher is tough, wait till you get a boss."

—

Bill Gates

"Your school may have done away with winners and losers, but life has not."

—

Bill Gates

"Like many others, I have deep misgivings about the state of education in the United States. Too many of our students fail to graduate from high school with the basic skills they will need to succeed in the 21st Century economy, much less prepared for the rigors of college and career. Although our top universities continue to rank among the best in the world, too few American students are pursuing degrees in science and technology. Compounding this problem is our failure to provide sufficient training for those already in the workforce."

—

Bill Gates

"Even though I only have a high-school degree, I'm a professional student."

—

Narendra Modi

"If there is education, there will be everything in life. Government can make roads, hospitals and also construct school buildings. But your homes can brighten up only if your children are educated. I am confident that if we focus on education, our society will certainly develop."

—

Marva Collins

"There is a brilliant child locked inside every student."

—

Marva Collins

"I'm a teacher. A teacher is someone who leads. There is no magic here. I do not walk on water. I do not part the sea. I just love children."

—

Marva Collins

"Kids don't fail. Teachers fail, school systems fail. The people who teach children that they are failures, they are the problem."

—

Marva Collins

"Once children learn how to learn, nothing is going to narrow their mind."

—

Marva Collins

"Students do not need to be labeled or measured any more than they are. They don't need more Federal funds, grants, and gimmicks. What they need from us is common sense, dedication, and bright, energetic teachers who believe that all children are achievers. And who take personally the failure of any one child."

—

Marva Collins

"Our children learn the phonetic method, which is why they're very good spellers, I suppose. Because rather than ABC or just saying a word, they'll have to go a, as in apple and all the other a's there are in the English language. They learn that when they're four. Children all over America can tell you that a, e, i, o, u, and sometimes y are vowels. But you ask them about that "sometimes y," and they can't tell you."

—

Marva Collins

"We've been brainwashed into thinking that it takes more monies than it actually does to educate children. That's been one of the brainwash jobs."

Marva Collins

"You can't find me 20 children in Chicago, I don't care which section you go in - you can be on Michigan Avenue or here - and they won't be able to tell you that y is a vowel when it's the final syllable in a word, as in Nancy and icy. And no one bothers to teach the rules anymore - "i before e except after c."

Marva Collins

"The more monies we spend, the less children learn; because the more machines we have there, the more gadgets, the more gimmicks, the less children have to really think - the less they have to use their innate abilities, their curiosity, their brains."

Marva Collins

"Teaching children to read was one thing; keeping them interested in reading was something else."

Stephen Covey

"But with the steady disintegration of the family in modern society over the last century, the role of the school in bridging the gap has become vital!"

—

Stephen Covey

"Historically, the family has played the primary role in educating children for life, with the school providing supplemental scaffolding to the family."

—

Stephen Covey

"Reducing children to a test score is the worst form of identity theft we could commit in schools."

—

Stephen Covey

"In this knowledge-worker age, it's now increasingly tied to doing well in school so you can get into better grad schools so you can get better jobs - so the pressure to do well is really high."

—

Jonathan Kozol

"I have been criticized throughout the course of my career for placing too much faith in the reliability of children's narratives; but I have almost always found that children are a great deal more reliable in telling us what actually goes on in public school than many of the adult experts who develop policies that shape their destinies."

—

Jonathan Kozol

"Good teachers don't approach a child of this age with overzealousness or with destructive conscientiousness. They're not drill-masters in the military or floor managers in a production system. They are specialists in opening small packages. They give the string a tug but do it carefully. They don't yet know what's in the box. They don't know if it's breakable."

Jonathan Kozol

"There is something deeply hypocritical in a society that holds an inner-city child only eight years old "accountable" for her performance on a high-stakes standardized exam but does not hold the high officials of our government accountable for robbing her of what they gave their own kids six or seven years before."

—

Jonathan Kozol

"Instead of seeing these children for the blessings that they are, we are measuring them only by the standard of whether they will be future deficits or assets for our nation's competitive needs."

—

Beverly Cleary

"Children should learn that reading is pleasure, not just something that teachers make you do in school."

—

Thomas Sowell

"Apparently, almost anyone can do a better job of educating children than our so-called 'educators' in the public schools. Children who are home-schooled by their parents also score higher on tests than children educated in the public schools. ... Successful education shows what is possible, whether in charter schools, private schools, military schools or home-schooling. The challenge is to provide more escape hatches from failing public schools, not only to help those students who escape but also to force these institutions to get their act together before losing more students and jobs."

—

Thomas Sowell

"Hilary Clinton said you know, it takes a village to raise a child and somebody said it takes a village idiot to believe that ... it is part of the whole thing of third parties wanting to make decisions for which they pay no price for when they're wrong."

—

Thomas Sowell

"Ours may become the first civilization destroyed, not by the power of our enemies, but by the ignorance of our teachers and the dangerous nonsense they are teaching our children. In an age of artificial intelligence, they are creating artificial stupidity."

—

Alice Waters

"Create a garden; bring children to farms for field trips. I think it's important that parents and teachers get together to do one or two things they can accomplish well - a teaching garden, connecting with farms nearby, weave food into the curriculum."

—

Michelle Obama

"While budgets are tight right now, there are schools across the country that are showing that it doesn't take a whole lot of money or resources to give our kids the nutrition they deserve. What it does take, however, is effort. What it does take is imagination. What it does take is a commitment to our children's futures."

—

AT SCHOOL.

Five little Girls, sitting on a form,
Five little Girls, with lessons to learn;
Five little Girls, who, I'm afraid,
Won't know them a bit when they have to be said.

For little eyes are given to look
Anywhere else than on their book;
And little thoughts are given to stray
Anywhere—ever so far away.

The difference between school and LIFE?

In school, you're taught a lesson and then given a TEST.

In life, you're given a test that teaches you a LESSON.

Eat Your Veggies. Food.

Food is our longest relationship in life. We begin in the womb sharing what our mothers eat. Then we are born and when we're upset and cry, we get a clean diaper and food. Then as we grow up food continues to be a part of every emotion.

Celebrations, grief, family time, depression, comfort food, party food, you name it and we include food as part of the emotion. Good or bad doesn't really play a part here as this is so deeply ingrained in us it simply is part of who and what we are.

So, doesn't it make sense to help our children have the best and healthiest relationship possible with food?

Voldane Pelt

A REAL FOOD MANIFESTO!

EAT REAL FOOD
NOT PACKETS AND PROMISES
Change ONE little thing a week
DO THE BEST YOU CAN
TEACH & COOK WITH YOUR KIDS
INSIST ON ETHICAL
GROW YOUR OWN
COOK FROM THE ♡
QUIT EATING NUMB3RS
Celebrate food together
SAY A LOUD **NO!** TO GMO
SUPPORT LOCAL FARMS
SPREAD THE WORD!

Alice Waters

"I think America's food culture is embedded in fast-food culture. And the real question that we have is: How are we going to teach slow-food values in a fast-food world? Of course, it's very, very difficult to do, especially when children have grown up eating fast food and the values that go with that."

—

Julia Child

"It's fun to get together and have something good to eat at least once a day. That's what human life is all about - enjoying things."

—

Jamie Oliver

"Real food doesn't have ingredients, real food is ingredients."

—

Alice Waters

"Good food is a right, not a privilege. It brings children into a positive relationship with their health, community, and environment."

—

Alice Waters

"We have to bring children into a new relationship to food that connects them to culture and agriculture."

—

Phyllis Diller

"My cooking is so bad my kids thought Thanksgiving was to commemorate Pearl Harbor."

—

Alice Waters

"I want every child in America to eat a nutritious, delicious, sustainably sourced school lunch for free."

—

Alice Waters

"Change the food in the schools and we can influence how children think. Change the curriculum and teach them how to garden and how to cook and we can show that growing food and cooking and eating together give lasting richness, meaning, and beauty to our lives."

—

Fran Lebowitz

"Ask your child what he wants for dinner only if he's buying."

—

Fran Lebowitz

"Breakfast cereals that come in the same colors as polyester leisure suits make oversleeping a virtue."

—

Fran Lebowitz

"Raisins are a thing that lasts, they come in small boxes, and you always feel like eating raisins, even at six in the morning. A raisin is always an appropriate snack."

—

Jamie Oliver

"Imagine a world where children were fed tasty and nutritious, real food at school from the age of 4 to 18. A world where every child was educated about how amazing food is, where it comes from, how it affects the body and how it can save their lives."

—

Jamie Oliver

"I wish for everyone to help create a strong, sustainable movement to educate every child about food, inspire families to cook again and empower people everywhere to fight obesity."

—

Jamie Oliver

"Every child should be taught to cook in school, not just talk about nutrition all day. Good food can be made in 15 minutes. This could be the first generation where the kids teach the parents."

—

Jamie Oliver

"I never get tired of talking about food. I do getting tired of fighting governments when they are so clearly not putting the best interest of the children forward."

—

Stephanie Klein

"It's about not rewarding your children with food, not always celebrating with food. I do think it's important to find other ways to comfort our children and ourselves, to work other ways of celebrating and rewarding."

—

Erma Bombeck

"The age of your children is a key factor in how quickly you are served in a restaurant. We once had a waiter in Canada who said, 'Could I get you your check?' and we answered, 'How about the menu first?'"

—

Erma Bombeck

"My son would walk to the refrigerator-freezer and fling both doors open and stand there until the hairs in his nose iced up. After surveying $200 worth of food in varying shapes and forms, he would declare loudly, 'There's nothing to eat!'"

—

Erma Bombeck

"It is ludicrous to read the microwave direction on the boxes of food you buy, as each one will have a disclaimer: THIS WILL VARY WITH YOUR MICROWAVE. Loosely translated, this means, You're on your own, Bernice."

—

Erma Bombeck

"Mother's words of wisdom: Answer me! Don't talk with food in your mouth!"

—

Erma Bombeck

"Maybe you know why a child can reject a hot dog with mustard served on a soft bun at home, yet eat six of them two hours later at fifty cents each."

—

Eric Schlosser

"The executives who run the fast-food industry are not bad men. They are businessmen. They will sell free-range, organic, grass-fed hamburgers if you demand it. They will sell whatever sells at a profit."

—

Eric Schlosser

"In 1970, Americans spent about $6 billion on fast food; in 2000, they spent more than $110 billion. Americans now spend more money on fast food than on higher education, personal computers, computer software, or new cars. They spend more on fast food than on movies, books, magazines, newspapers, videos, and recorded music combined."

—

Robert Orben

"Remember the days when you let your child have some chocolate if he finished his cereal? Now, chocolate is one of the cereals."

—

Pope Francis

"If in so many parts of the world there are children who have nothing to eat, that's not news, it seems normal. It cannot be this way!"

—

W. C. Fields

"There's no such thing as a tough child - if you parboil them first for seven hours, they always come out tender."

—

W. C. Fields

"My illness is due to my doctor's insistence that I drink milk, a whitish fluid they force down helpless babies."

—

Jane Bown

"Failing to provide children adequate access to nutritious food not only endangers their emotional, physical and mental development, but it also puts all aspects of their future well-being at risk. The costs are too high when you short-change children."

—

Samantha Harris

"Food insecurity and hunger are serious threats to children's health, growth, and development. The idea of not being able to put plentiful, nutritious food on the table for my girls is a horrifying thought."

—

Anna Lappe

"The food industry is spending almost $2 billion a year marketing directly to children and teens. We know that those ads lead to children demanding certain brands, and we know that food and drink marketing gets all of us to consume more calories. If we're going to address diet-related illnesses, talking about marketing to kids is a key step. There should be places like schools that are protected sanctuaries from commercialization and from advertising, especially when it comes to kids' health."

—

Quotes for Parents

Michelle Obama

"Some kids have never seen what a real tomato looks like off the vine. They don't know where a cucumber comes from. And that really affects the way they view food. So, a garden helps them really get their hands dirty, literally, and understand the whole process of where their food comes from. And I wanted them to see just how challenging and rewarding it is to grow your own food, so that they would better understand what our farmers are doing every single day across this country and have an appreciation for ... that American tradition of growing our own food and feeding ourselves."

—

Michelle Obama

"It's not about government telling people what to do. It's about each of us, in our own families, in our own communities, standing up and demanding more for our kids. And it's about companies like Walmart answering that call."

—

P. J. O'Rourke

"Vegetables are something God invented to let women get even with their children."

—

Rick Santorum

"I watch the Food Network with my kids. We - yeah, I - I - I generally don't admit that, but I love cooking."

—

Tom Aikens

"Kids get very animated when it comes to food and it's nice to see how they react."

—

Melanie Charlene

"Children who grow what they eat will often eat what they grow"

—

Meryl Streep

"It's bizarre that the produce manager is more important to my children's health than the pediatrician."

—

E. B. White (1899-1985)

"MOTHER: It's broccoli, dear.

CHILD: I say it's spinach, and I say the hell with it."

—

Barbara Costikyan

"In the childhood memories of every good cook, there's a large kitchen, a warm stove, a simmering pot, and a mom."

—

Garrison Keillor

"The highlight of my childhood was making my brother laugh so hard that food came out of his nose."

—

Katherine Whitehorn

"A food is not necessarily essential just because your child hates it."

—

Eric Pritchard

"As a rule, children dislike foods which are said to be good for them or are forced on them, and they take strong fancies to foods which they are not allowed to eat; advantage should be taken of these tendencies."

—

Guy Fieri

"Preparing food is one of life's great joys, but a lot of times, parents ask their kids if they want to cook with them and then tell them to go peel a bag of potatoes. That's not cooking – that's working!"

—

Emeril Lagasse

"When I cook with my son, I might chop vegetables and have fun with different shapes. Cooking is a way to teach kids about other things, like reading or math with all of the weights and measures. There are so many things that are part of cooking that are also very educational."

—

Guy Fieri

"Cooking with kids is not just about ingredients, recipes, and cooking. It's about harnessing imagination, empowerment, and creativity."

—

Tom Douglas

"Cooking with your kids is a remarkable exercise to let them in on the purchasing part of the process – kids love to shop, and it's great to take them to these ethnic places where people don't always speak the language."

—

Mario Batali

"Working at the Food Bank with my kids is an eye-opener. The face of hunger isn't the bum on the street drinking Sterno; it's the working poor. They don't look any different, they don't behave any differently, they're not really any less educated. They are incredibly less privileged, and that's it."

—

Cat Cora

"We incorporated new tastes and flavors into our kids' diets from a very early age, which helped to develop their palates and prevented them from becoming picky eaters. We don't buy junk food and give them options of fresh fruit, yogurt, raw almonds, or dried whole grain cereals for snack time."

—

Cat Cora

"When I was growing up in Mississippi - it was good Southern food... but I also grew up with a Greek family; when other kids were eating fried okra, we were eating steamed artichokes. So, I think it played a big part in my healthy cooking."

—

Guy Fieri

"Short of screaming-hot Thai food, everything can be suitable for kids too."

Felicity Huffman

"Between work and the kids, I never see anyone anymore. I mean, when I first met with ABC last spring, and they asked me what I'd been doing lately, I said: 'Gee, I have two kids. I'm usually covered with food, wrinkled and feel guilty all the time."

Morgan Spurlock

"The food is absolutely atrocious, and parents have no idea. Parents are giving their kids three dollars and saying, 'Okay, see you later. Go off to school and have a good lunch."

Curtis Stone

"In my travels, I also noticed that kids in Thailand like spicy food and kids in India love curry. I'm hoping to introduce my son, Hudson, to lots of veggies and spices when he's young. I say that before he's started on solid foods, so it could be easier in theory than practice!"

Alice Waters

"The fact that most kids aren't eating at home with their families any more really means they are eating elsewhere. They are eating out there in fast-food nation."

Alice Waters

"First, kids should be involved in the production of their own food. They have to get their hands in the dirt, they have to grow things. They also have to become sensually stimulated, and the way to begin is with a bakery."

Chuck Norris

"Getting kids into the kitchen preparing the food they and their families will eat results in them viewing food in an entirely new way. If given the right ingredients, that act alone can raise the standards of the quality of the food both they and their family eat."

Donald Driver

"My kids know there's no candy, no soda, until the weekend. Those are the days they get to indulge in their sweets. We're big on organic food. I'm not a diet guy; I don't believe in diets. I just believe in a great meal plan."

—

Graham Elliot

"Kids see cooking as a creative outlet now, like soccer and ballet. It gives me hope that things like fast food, childhood obesity and the horrible state of school lunches can be addressed by kids and their parents."

—

Joel Robuchon

"A few years ago, kids from poor areas in France were asked to draw items of food. For a chicken, they drew a drumstick. For a fish, they drew a fish stick. Those are extremes, but there is a lot that needs to be done to help children discover good food."

—

Joey Fatone

"I'm Italian. I love to cook Italian food, so I learned from my dad how to make sauce and meatballs and all that stuff. With my wife and kids, I started making homemade pasta. The very first time, I didn't have a pasta maker, so I had to cut it with a knife, the old-school way! The noodles were all jacked up, but it was fun."

—

Jorge Cruise

"You have to be a mindful eater. There has to be intention in what you do in your life if you're going to be happy and authentic. Food isn't supposed to be entertainment in the way that your kids, your work, and your relationship are."

—

Letitia Baldrige

"Kids today and for the last 20 years have held the fork and knife in unbelievable ways. They hold the fork with a fist and the knife like a saw and they shovel it in. It doesn't matter to them which way they hold their knife and fork. They eat every which way. I'm amazed they get food into their mouths at all."

—

Louis C. K.

"When two kids are being completely berserk, and they're naked and throwing food around, sometimes I just let it go because I can see a future where they're going to be dressed, and they're going to be at school. So, I kind of let stuff go sometimes."

—

Lisa Ling

"Parents are working more than ever before and unable to monitor what kids are eating at home, and schools are selling astronomical amounts of junk food in order to supplement shrinking budgets. It's a ticking time bomb, and America's children are exploding."

—

Kimbal Musk

"The problem is that restaurants have assumed that kids don't want to eat anything other than chicken nuggets or fast-food burgers, but they do. They want to eat things that taste good."

—

Kimbal Musk

"We want kids in communities to know real food, and we want them to have a choice between real food and industrial food."

—

Kourtney Kardashian

"My mom fed us a lot of processed food when we were kids, like chicken fingers, grilled cheese sandwiches, and quesadillas. I make those treats for my family, too, but I use organic cheeses and whole wheat bread and tortillas."

—

K. A. Applegate

"It occurred to me that a food drive would be a natural way to talk to kids about hunger, which so many of them simply aren't aware of."

—

Marcus Samuelsson

"Cooking with your kids and engaging them in hands-on activities are two ways to begin to educate children about the healthy eating, and kick start the important task to help change how the younger generation looks at food and nutrition."

—

Peter Senge

"There's a lot of American kids think their food comes from the grocery store and the concept of seasonality has no meaning to them whatsoever."

—

Ruth Reichl

"The way we allow children to be advertised to is shocking. Eating is a learned behavior, and we've made these kids sitting ducks for all the bad messages about industrialized food. The fact that we allow that to go on is horrifying."

—

Rebecca Stead

My kids really like food, and they like to cook, so it's a lot of fun to shop with them."

—

Erma Bombeck

In general, my children refuse to eat anything that hasn't danced in television.

—

A baby will make love stronger, days shorter, nights longer, bank rolls shorter, home happier, clothes shabbier, the past forgotten, and the future worth living for.

Raising children is like making biscuits: it is easy to raise a big batch as one; while you have your hands in the dough.
E.W. Howe

The First Art of being a parent CONSISTS OF SLEEPING WHEN THE BABY ISN'T LOOKING

Life with kiddos

From the moment you bring the child home nothing is ever the same. You think that your body swelling to the size of a full moon or your significant others body doing the swelling while you watch like a deer in the headlights is a change.

Forget about it. Kiddos change everything and while most of its wonderful some of it smells bad, destroys your home, gives you grey hair and heartburn. But in the end, if we live through those parts, we get to share their lives and what a wonderous trip that is.

En

This chapter pokes fun as well as gives some insight into how other parents cope with miniature tornados running around.

Voldane Pelt

"Look up at the stars and not down at your feet. Try to make sense of what you see, and wonder about what makes the universe exist. Be curious."

- Stephen Hawking

Ray Romano

"Having children is like living in a frat house - nobody sleeps, everything's broken, and there's a lot of throwing up."

—

William Martin

"Do not ask your children to strive for extraordinary lives. Such striving may seem admirable, but it is the way of foolishness. Help them instead to find the wonder and the marvel of an ordinary life. Show them the joy of tasting tomatoes, apples and pears. Show them how to cry when pets and people die. Show them the infinite pleasure in the touch of a hand. And make the ordinary come alive for them. The extraordinary will take care of itself."

—

Margaret Culkin Banning

"Cleaning up with children around is like shoveling during a blizzard"

—

Glennon Melton

"Don't let yourself become so concerned with raising a good kid that you forget you already have one."

—

Milton Berle

"If evolution really works, how come mothers only have two hands?"

—

Bil Keane

"OF COURSE, I'd like to be the ideal mother. But I'm too busy raising children."

—

Jackie Chan

"Since the child knew his parents would give in, he tried the same trick again and again."

—

Thomas Sowell

"How are children supposed to learn to act like adults, when so much of what they see on television shows adults acting like children?"

—

Thomas Sowell

"Even if her children or grandchildren are willing to spend their own money to keep grandma alive, when bureaucrats control the necessary technology or medication, they may decide that it is not for sale."

—

Fran Lebowitz

"Even when freshly washed and relieved of all obvious confections, children tend to be sticky."

—

Robert Orben

"Do your kids a favor - don't have any."

—

Robert Orben

"I take my children everywhere, but they always find their way back home."

—

Socrates

"Children today are tyrants. They contradict their parents, gobble their food, and tyrannize their teachers."

—

Erma Bombeck

"Never have more children than you have car windows."

—

Dr. Seuss

"A person's a person, no matter how small."

—

Voldane Pelt

This next one made me remember the game of repeating everything I said to her and she repeated back. Somehow, I do not

think she was listening to what she said any more than when I said it the first time.

—

Jane Nelsen

"Children will listen to you after they feel listened to."

—

Franklin P. Jones

"You can learn many things from children. How much patience you have, for instance?"

—

Margaret Mead

"Children must be taught how to think, not what to think."

—

Muhammad Ali

"Children make you want to start life over."

—

Albert Einstein

"If you want your children to be intelligent, read them fairy tales. If you want them to be more intelligent, read them more fairy tales."

—

Henny Youngman

"What is a home without children? Quiet."

—

Joseph Joubert

"Children need models rather than critics."

—

Anne Frank

"Even if people are still very young, they shouldn't be prevented from saying what they think."

—

Hodding Carter

"There are only two lasting bequests we can hope to give our children. One is roots; the other, wings."

—

Plato

"Let parents bequeath to their children not riches, but the spirit of reverence."

—

Pam Brown

"Always smile back at little children. To ignore them is to destroy their belief that the world is good."

—

Pablo Picasso

"It took me four years to paint like Raphael, but a lifetime to paint like a child."

—

Neil Gaiman

"Adults follow paths. Children explore."

Dr. Seuss

"Adults are just outdated children."

—

Johnny Depp

"When kids hit 1 year old, it's like hanging out with a miniature drunk. You have to hold onto them. They bump into things. They laugh and cry. They urinate. They vomit."

—

Aristotle

"Mothers are fonder than fathers of their children because they are more certain they are their own."

—

Ralph Waldo Emerson

"A child is a curly dimpled lunatic."

—

Jill Bensley

"The most effective form of birth control I know is spending the day with my kids."

—

Jennifer James

"The first half of our lives is spoiled by our parents and the last half by our children."

—

Doug Dillon

"A child's imaginary playmate just might actually be there."

—

Voldane Pelt

It's all adult fun until the condom breaks, then it's all kinds of childish fun.

—

Ben Bergor

"It is amazing how quickly the kids learn to drive a car, yet are unable to understand the lawnmower, snow-blower or vacuum cleaner."

—

John Ruskin

"Children are a great comfort to us in our old age, and they help us reach it faster too."

—

Colin Egglesfield

"The reason I love kids so much is because, they're so honest, so you know right away if they like you or they don't."

—

Robin Williams

"I love kids, but they are a tough audience."

—

Rodney Dangerfield

"When I was a kid my parents moved a lot, but I always found them."

Walt Streightiff

"There are no seven wonders of the world in the eyes of a child. There are seven million."

Charles Osgood

"Babies are always more trouble than you thought and more wonderful."

Bill Maher

"I don't dislike children; I just don't particularly want to be around with them a lot. Problem is, neither do their parents."

Jo Brand

"No one I know is actually so rude as to tell me I've become duller since having children. But I'm sure they think it."

Quotes for Parents

Will Ferrell

"Once a person has a child, the first question everyone asks is: "Are you going to have more children?" But it basically means: "Are you going to have more sex with your wife in the hopes of having children?""

—

Jill Hennessy

"I've found it easier to write, to coalesce my thoughts, since having children. It brings you back to what you experienced yourself as a child, and you empathize with what your parents went through."

—

Paul Reiser

"The first time I tried to put a new diaper on my baby, I yanked the little Velcro strap too jerkily and actually punched the little guy in the jaw. A real solid shot, too. I knew instinctively that this could not be correct. Unless you're specifically trying to raise a welterweight, continual deliverance of powerful uppercuts is not advised when handling newborns."

Paul Reiser

"Get a good dog. We have not picked up food in the kitchen in 15 years."

Quotes for Parents

Dating & Kids

For whatever the reason at some point we end up dating even people who are not parents usually wind up, dating at least a few people in their lives who are parents. And even if you avoid the dating someone with children eventually your children end up dating someone else's children.

Dating is hard enough today that most of us do not want to make it any harder than it already is. Yet when you have children at some point, they will have a say and then some about you dating.

These quotes will make you smile, a few might give some tips but for the most, they will help you remember that parents have been dating for decades and society has survived. We usually end up with more grey hairs than before, but dating can do that even without kids.

Voldane Pelt

Voldane Pelt

I have dated a few women who had kids that this would have been a relief.

—

Rodney Dangerfield

"One woman I was dating called and said, 'Come on over, there's nobody home.' I went over. Nobody was home."

—

Rita Rudner

"Whenever I date a guy, I think, "Is this the man I want my children to spend their weekends with?"

—

Michelle Landry

"My mom always complains about my lack of a boyfriend. Well, next time she asks, I'm going to tell her I'm dating two different guys — Mr. Duracell and Mr. Energizer."

—

"INTRODUCE A NEW PARTNER ONLY IF YOU FEEL IT IS A SIGNIFICANT RELATIONSHIP. CHILDREN DO NOT NEED TO MEET EVERY MAN YOU DATE. YOU ARE YOUR CHILDREN'S ROLE MODEL; YOU WANT THEM TO HAVE A POSITIVE OUTLOOK ON RELATIONSHIPS AND FEEL STABILITY AND A SENSE OF SECURITY."

Judy Carter

"About age 30 most women think about having children, most men think about dating them."

—

Voldane Pelt

As sad as the joint custody can often be it helps to look at the upside.

—

Delia Ephron

"As complicated as joint custody is, it allows the delicious contradiction of having children and maintaining the intimacy of life-before-kids."

—

Paul Reiser

"Our date-night rule is no talking about the kids. That lasts about to the end of the driveway."

—

Paul Reiser

"I used to walk into a party and scan the room for attractive women. Now I look for women to hold my baby so I can eat potato salad sitting down."

—

Chelsea Handler

"The only thing worse than dating a single mom is dating a single mom that won't put out."

—

Andre Dubus III

"Years later I would hear my father say the divorce had left him dating his children. That still meant picking us up every Sunday for a matinee and, if he had the money, an early dinner somewhere."

—

Harville Hendrix

"Many divorced or widowed people do with their singleness what they should have done before they married for the first time: live alone, find their own rhythms, date a variety of people, go into therapy, develop new friends and interests, learn how to live with and care for themselves."

Dan Pearce

"The most difficult part of dating as a single parent is deciding how much risk your own child's heart is worth.

—

Priscilla Presley

"You know, I had my mother and my father convincing me that he would be going back to Hollywood and he'd be back with the actresses and dating them and that he wasn't serious about me at all. So, I had him saying one thing to me and my parents telling me something else."

—

Jim Bishop

"Watching your daughter being collected by her date feels like handing over a million-dollar Stradivarius to a gorilla."

—

Bill Engvall

"I pulled the boy close to me and said 'You see that girl, that's my only lil' girl. So, if you think about huggin' or kissin'. Remember these words. I ain't afraid to go back to prison'."

—

Voldane Pelt

Hot Tip for keeping teens home and not out dating.

—

Dorothy Parker

"The best way to keep children at home is to make the home atmosphere pleasant, and let the air out of the tires."

—

Voldane Pelt

When they begin dating, I think is the warning sign from one to the other. Good luck.

—

Mary Margaret McBride

"There is no time so short as the time between when your kids stop wrecking your furniture and your grandchildren start."

—

Cinco Paul

"I remember when my daughter was twelve, suddenly a boy started hanging out in front of our house after school. It was this kid, Justin. My office at the time was right in the front, so I just looked out the window. I couldn't write. I couldn't concentrate. I was like, 'What are you doing? What do you expect to achieve by standing in front of my house with my daughter inside?' I hated that kid so much."

—

Voldane Pelt

Close to dating with kids and a duck come on I had to include it.

—

Lea Thompson

"My kids can't watch ('*Howard the Duck*'). By the time I get in bed with the duck, they are, like,

'Turn it off, mom. You in bed with a duck' is just pretty much a deal-breaker."

—

Kami Garcia

"And have her back by midnight. "

"Is that some powerful Caster hour?"

"No. It's her curfew."

—

Tim McGraw

"I have three daughters, so I can't be as tough as I want to be. When you have kids - especially daughters - they know how to work you. They're a lot smarter than we are, that's for sure. But I'll be more tough on their boyfriends."

—

Catherine Gilbert Murdock

"And have your mother put my head on a stake? Do you have any notion what that would do to my handsome good looks?"

—

John Scalzi

"When you're a teenager and you're in love, it's obvious to everyone but you and the person you're in love with."

—

Anonymous Author

"Imagination is something that sits up with Dad and Mom the first time their teenager stays out late."

—

Judith Martin

"Chaperons don't enforce morality; they force immorality to be discreet."

—

Bob Phillips

"Teenagers complain there's nothing to do, then stay out all night doing it."

—

Author Unknown

"A babysitter is a teenager acting like an adult while the adults are out acting like teenagers."

—

Voldane Pelt

As parents together or single this one is important. Ladies sometimes date night is a glass of wine, a toy and rechargeable batteries, that recharge faster than Viagra works.

—

Kevin Leman

"A fulfilling sex life is one of the most powerful marital glues a couple can have."

—

Kevin Leman

"A sexually fulfilled husband will do anything for you."

—

Matthew Stout
Date night?

—

Kate Beckinsale

"I'm very blessed to have a husband who appreciates me. Women feel sexy from feeling attractive and desired. Men feel sexy from having sex. If you can strike a balance where the man is having sex a lot and the woman is feeling desired enough to have sex, then you've figured out the secret to a marriage that's alive."

—

Jeff Foxworthy

"You might be a redneck if you dated your daddy's current wife in high school."

—

Antonio Banderas

"I wouldn't want my daughters to date a guy like me. I was dangerous around women in my twenties. I'm terrified that they might end up with someone like me."

Anna Benson

"I'm very traditional, believe it or not. My daughters are not allowed to date until they're at least 16 and I'm going to make it 18 for the next one."

Matthew Stout

Just for a laugh.

Bob Saget

"Soon, I'm going to meet somebody around my own age, and she's going to be smart and beautiful, and I'm going to date her daughter."

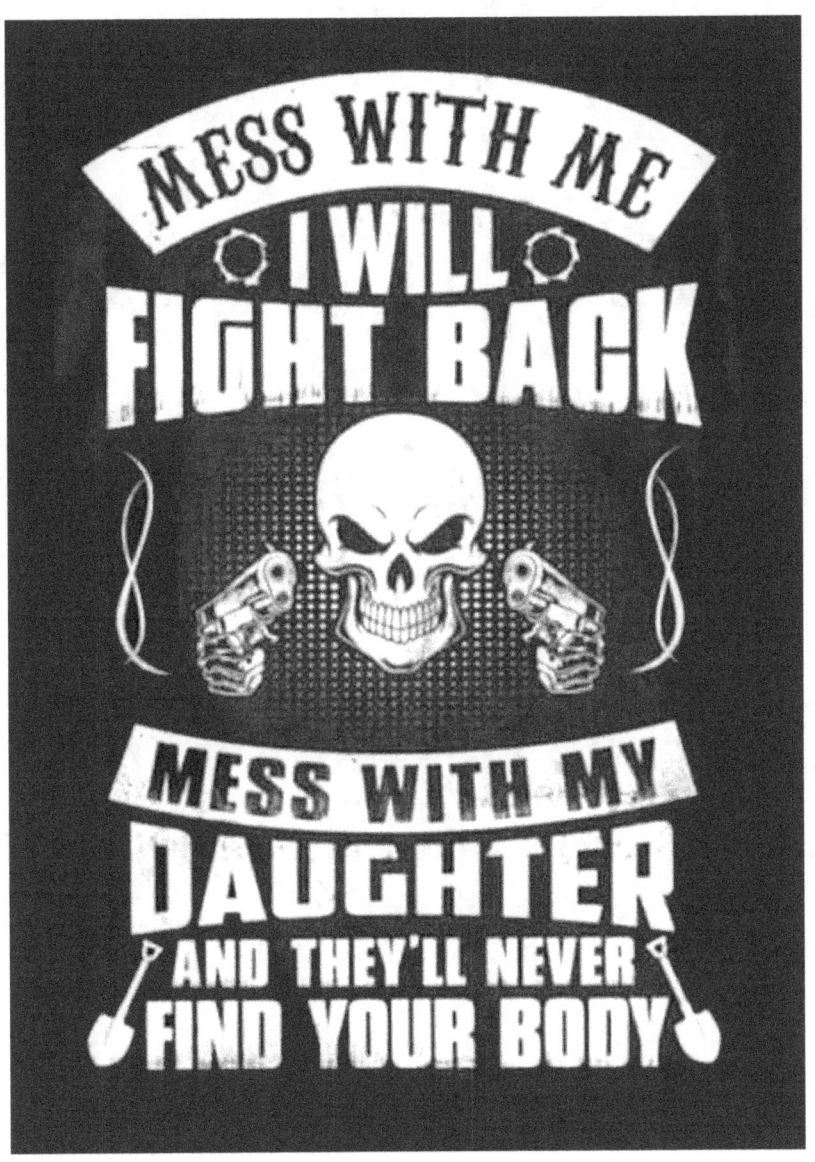

Anyone can have a child and call themselves "a parent". A real parent is someone who puts that child above their own selfish needs and wants.

The Birds & the Bees - Safe Sex? Uh... here read this.

SEX! It is how you ended up a parent but somehow discussing it with the product of that sex is just doesn't seem natural or as much fun. I am sure there are out there in the world a few parents who do find chatting about sex and all it entails in today's world with no qualms.

For the rest of us it's an important, awkward oft time scary and as potentially hilarious as a disastrous act that our minds scream, "Uh here read this, ask the teacher or mom or dad." These quotes are ofttimes crude, funny, and some really say stuff that we should think about.

You will not and I do not agree with all of these quotes or those that said them. The ones I found most out there from my beliefs still made me think and thinking is important. So, I hope these make you laugh, think and be there for the big kids' questions that they can't find the words to ask.

—

Voldane Pelt

> "Women need a reason to have sex. Men just need a place."
>
> Billy Crystal

Martin Amis

"My 12-year-old daughter said to me, 'Enough with the subtitles, Daddy, for crying out loud.' Because they always seem to cloud the issue rather than clarify it."

—

Kyra Sedgwick

"I'm going to embarrass my kids - sex is important. Sex is really important."

—

Anonymous

"You can tell a child is growing up when he stops asking where he came from and starts refusing to tell where he is going."

—

Will Rogers

"I never expected to see the day when girls would get sunburned in the places they do now."

—

Fran Lebowitz

"Don't bother discussing sex with small children. They rarely have anything to add."

—

Arnold H. Glasow

"Telling a teenager, the facts of life is like giving a fish a bath."

—

C Pulsifer

"Keeping that communication channel open with your teen is one of the most important things as a parent you can do."

—

William H. Masters

"The best sex education for kids is when Daddy pats Mommy on the fanny when he comes home from work."

—

Madalyn Murray O'Hair

"Kids should be taught about sex, sex hygiene and contraceptive methods starting in the sixth grade, and whenever they want to try it, they should be allowed to go at it without supervision or restriction -in their parents' bedroom, on the grass in a park, in a motel; it doesn't matter, as long as the setting is private and pleasant. If we did all this, our kids would grow up into happier, healthier human beings. But we won't, of course. It would make too much sense."

—

Pat Paulsen

"In opposition to sex education: Let the kids today learn it where we did - in the gutter."

—

Milton Berle

"I don't worry too much about sex education in the schools. If the kids learn it like they do everything else, they won't know-how."

—

Phyllis Schlafly

Quotes for Parents

"Sex education classes are like in-home sales parties for abortions."

—

Mary Sue Terry

"I was raised in a small town. It was so small that our school taught driver's education and sex education in the same car."

—

Susie Bright

"My idea of the ideal sex education site doesn't exist."

—

Wendy Davis

"Let's make sure that we are working for age-appropriate sex education in our school system."

—

Voldane Pelt

This next one made me stop and think. So, let's say a kid is into feet - like feet excite

him, and in his mind, they are the equivalent of a nude beach. Does that make first base painting toenails? If so, I bet that kid would be really popular with the girls.

—

Donna Shalala

"Sex education has to do with what's in people's head."

—

Sue Johanson

"Kids and adults have sex for many, many reasons... Put out a question box."

—

James Dobson

"One of the problems with sex education... is that it also strips kids - especially girls - of their modesty to have every detail of anatomy, physiology and condom usage made explicit."

—

Sandra Bernhard

"Kids need to be educated about sex and sexuality and if they're going to have sex, learn how to protect themselves and not get pregnant."

—

Benjamin Spock

"Sex education, including its spiritual aspects, should be part of a broad health and moral education from kindergarten through grade twelve, ideally carried out harmoniously by parents and teachers."

—

Sue Johanson

"Sex is... perfectly natural. It's something that's pleasurable. It's enjoyable and it enhances a relationship. So why don't we learn as much as we can about it and become comfortable with ourselves as sexual human beings because we are all sexual?"

—

Benjamin Spock

"Does sex education encourage sex? Many parents are afraid that talking about sex with their teenagers will be taken as permission for the teen to have sex. Nothing could be further from the truth. If anything, the more children learn about sexuality from talking with their parents and teachers and reading accurate books, the less they feel compelled to find out for themselves."

—

Bertrand Russell

"Answering questions is a major part of sex education. Two rules cover the ground. First, always give a truthful answer to a question; secondly, regard sex knowledge as exactly like any other knowledge."

—

Albert Einstein

"Regarding sex education: no secrets!"

—

Elayne Boosler

"People want sex education out of the schools. They believe sex education causes promiscuity. Hey, I took algebra, but I never do math."

Mal Fletcher

"Sex education should be 'relationship education', focusing on how to achieve long-term commitment."

Bruno Bettelheim

"You cannot have sex education without saying that sex is natural and that most people find it pleasurable."

Piers Anthony

"In fact, I believe that we need better sex education in our own culture, here in America, so that young folk learn about things like venereal disease before they encounter it."

Phyllis Schlafly

"What masquerades as sex education is not education at all. It is selective propaganda which artificially encourages children to participate in adult sex, while it censors out the facts of life about the unhappy consequences. It is robbing children of their childhood."

—

Sue Johanson

"Americans are a decade behind Canada when it comes to sex education and understanding their bodies."

—

Ashton Kutcher

"In the sex education process in schools, the one thing that they teach about is how to get pregnant and how to not get pregnant. But they don't really talk about sex as a point of pleasure for women."

—

Pepper Schwartz

"Parents aren't sex education experts just because they are parents."

—

> Sex is emotion in motion.
>
> Mae West

Richard Mitchell

"There is only one remedy for ignorance and thoughtlessness, and that is literacy. Millions and millions of children would today stand in no need of sex education or consumer education or anti-racism education or any of those fake educations if they had had in the first place 'an' education."

—

Beverly LaHaye

"One of the most devastating enemies of the family is radical sex education in the public school. It is more explicit than necessary for the good of the child. Too much sex education too soon causes undue curiosity and obsession with sex."

—

Karl Kraus

"Sex education is legitimate in that girls cannot be taught soon enough how children don't come into the world."

—

Jeanette Winterson

"The only sex education my mother ever gave me was the injunction: 'Never let a boy touch you down there.' I had no idea what she meant. She seemed to be referring to my knees."

—

Frankie Boyle

"When I went to school, sex education was mainly muttered warnings about the janitor."

—

Stockwell Day

"If the Liberals' law is passed, will sex education in the schools, including elementary grades, include the same portrayals of sexual activity which presently exist in heterosexual instruction? Will there be the same presentation of homosexual activity? Of course, there will."

—

Phyllis Schlafly

"The persistent advocates of contraceptive-style sex education have become more and more resourceful in using taxpayer funds to impose their casual-sex attitudes and explicit-sex instruction on other people's children."

—

Bill Ayers

"We have sex education - I'm for it, I'm not against it. But any curriculum should recognize that it's young people's job to invent it themselves. You're not going to teach them; they're going to reinvent it."

—

Victoria Wood

"In my day we didn't have sex education, we just picked up what we could off the television."

—

Jane Fonda

"I would think that if you understood what sex education is, you would get down on your knees and worship a condom."

—

Ann Coulter

"[Liberals] think they can pass a law eliminating guns and nuclear weapons, but teenagers having sex is completely beyond our control."

—

Natalie Portman

"Where I live, nobody who's fourteen is having sex and doing major drugs. And I think if you see it in the movies, you may be influenced by it. I think it's so important to preserve your innocence."

—

Voldane Pelt

Not sure kids would see the humor in this one so it must be funny.

—

Bill Maher

"Kids. They're not easy, but there has to be some penalty for having sex."

—

Sharon Stone

"When I'm with my friends' teenage children, I always say, 'Are your friends having sex yet?'"

—

Voldane Pelt

This should probably be part of sex education. Rather in a book, at school, home or whatever but kids should know about testing.

—

Jay Ellis

"We think that if we get tested, that means you have to have HIV. Or we think that just by knowing someone with HIV, we're going to get HIV or because he's gay or she's a lesbian or whatever. This false information has been put out there and it's created this stigma that stops us from going to find out if we're infected. The truth is it doesn't matter who you are, if you're having sex, you need to be getting tested, plain and simple."

—

Timothy Radcliffe

"Celibacy is not just a matter of not having sex. It is a way of admiring a person for their humanity, maybe even for their beauty."

—

Voldane Pelt

Now this one had me wondering if for months your teenager is a holy terror and the next day, they are happy angels if you should lose some condoms around the house. You know like the twenty they found in your jeans.

—

Jake LaMotta

"You can't go into the ring and be a nice guy. I would go a month, two months, without having sex. It worked for me because it made me a vicious animal. You can't fight if you have any compassion or anything like that."

—

Voldane Pelt

Quotes for Parents

When your kids say they know all about sex so shut up, ask them to prove it and answer this question.

—

William Carlos Williams

"You have the chicken, the hen, and the rooster. The chicken goes with the hen So who is having sex with the rooster?"

—

Nate Parker

"I'm 36-years-old and I'm learning about definitions that I should have known when I started having sex."

—

Voldane Pelt

An interesting idea to encourage condom use or just get some odd looks from your kids when you suggest it.

—

David Mazzucchelli

"Me? I like wearing a condom. It means I'm having sex. I already spend most of my time NOT wearing one. It's like a tuxedo - I enjoy putting one on for special occasions."

—

Jessica Valenti

"There were a WHOLE LOTTA us not having sex at Harvard . . . but none of us thought that that was special enough to start a club about it, for Pete's sake."

—

Voldane Pelt

If the kid asks the difference between sex and making love this is a good answer.

—

Gilbert Arenas

"Everyone is having sex until they fall in love. When you fall in love, then it's making love."

—

Voldane Pelt

I wonder if part of the young women today being with more partners is that they know sex should lead to orgasms, but no one shed any light on foreplay, and that for a young man helping her get there is like diffusing a bomb blindfolded. So, they just keep trying different partners looking for that big O.

—

Lizzy Caplan

"If you're raised in a household where questions are encouraged, you're the minority. It's sad. One of the things that has resonated the most for me is that, in the '50s, if your sex life was unfulfilling, it was your fault, as a woman. It was never the man's fault. Millions of women thought they were working with faulty equipment. If they couldn't have orgasms from having sex with their husbands, then they were broken. That's insane, and everybody believed it."

—

Bob Hope

"My father told me all about the birds and the bees, the liar - I went steady with a woodpecker till I was twenty-one."

George Bernard Shaw

"Instruction in sex is as important as instruction in food; yet not only are our adolescents not taught the physiology of sex, but never warned that the strongest sexual attraction may exist between persons so incompatible in tastes and capacities that they could not endure living together for a week much less a lifetime."

> **LOVE ISN'T ABOUT GRAND GESTURES, OR THE MOON AND THE STARS. IT'S JUST DUMB LUCK. AND SOMETIMES, YOU MEET SOMEONE WHO FEELS THE SAME WAY. AND THEN, SOMETIMES, YOU'RE UNLUCKY. BUT ONE DAY, YOU'RE GONNA MEET SOMEONE WHO APPRECIATES YOU FOR WHO YOU ARE. I MEAN, THERE'S SEVEN BILLION PEOPLE ON THE PLANET. I KNOW ONE OF THEM IS GONNA CLIMB UP ON A MOON FOR YOU.**
>
> — OTIS MILBURN

Toddlers

There are certain times during a child's life when things move at a super velocity. Everything is changing, new, and like all things that are fast a shooting star they are beautiful and like a tornado they can destroy your house, and everything still be sunny the next day.

This chapter of quotes is all about that time when toddlers are both beautiful, amazing and powerful tornados we can't let go of.

Voldane Pelt

Robert Benchley

"In America, there are two classes of travel first class and with children."

—

Janet Gonzalez-Mena

"Toddlers are active explorers. They eagerly try new things and use materials in different ways. Toddlers want to be independent and they have a strong sense of ownership."

—

Emma Watson

"It was unbelievable seeing me as an action figure! In a few months, toddlers all around the country will be biting my head off!"

—

Erma Bombeck

"When my kids become wild and unruly, I use a nice, safe playpen. When they're finished, I climb out."

—

Penelope Leach

"Your toddler will be 'good' if he feels like doing what you happen to want him to do and does not happen to feel like doing anything you would dislike. With a little cleverness, you can organize life as a whole, and issues in particular so that you both want the same thing most of the time."

—

Louise J. Kaplan

"As he walks away on his own two feet--the toddler's body-mind has reached its moment of perfection. The world is his and he the mighty conqueror of all he beholds... As long as mother sticks around in the wings, the mighty acrobat confidently performs his trick of twirling in circles, walking on tiptoe, jumping, climbing, staring, naming. He is joyous, filled with his grandeur and wondrous omnipotence."

—

Neil deGrasse Tyson

"And extracting one molecule's signature in spectral analysis from the rest of the signatures is hard work, sort of like picking out the sound of your toddler's voice in a roomful of screaming children during playtime. It's hard, but you can do it."

—

Michael Nesmith

"Just because you can thrill a toddler by chewing with your mouth open "doesn't mean you should."

—

Emily Oster

"The basic idea that incentives can be used to motivate behavior is a powerful one. It works for employees, and it has a clear place in parenting, as anyone who has tried to potty-train a recalcitrant toddler with sticker rewards knows."

—

Penelope Leach

"A preschool child does not emerge from your toddler on a given date or birthday. He becomes a child when he ceases to be a wayward, confusing, unpredictable and often balky person-in-the-making and becomes a comparatively cooperative, eager-and-easy-to-please real human being--at least 60 percent of the time."

—

Jan Hunt

"Toddlers ask many questions, and so do school children - until about grade three. By that time, many of them have learned an unfortunate fact, that in school, it can be more important for self-protection to hide one's ignorance about a subject than to learn more about it, regardless of one's curiosity."

—

Bruno Bettelheim

"As Anna Freud remarked, the toddler who wanders off into some other aisle feels lost, and screams anxiously for his mother, never says 'I got lost,' but accusingly says 'You lost me!' It is a rare mother who agrees that she lost him! She expects her child to stay with her; in her experience, it is the child who has lost track of the mother, while in the child's experience it is the mother who has lost track of him. Each view is entirely correct from the perspective of the individual who holds it."

Natasha Leggero

"TLC should stand for Toddlers, Lunatics, and Cake."

Devra Davis

"The reality is, cellphones have to be used safely. They are today like cars and trucks - we can't live without them, but we certainly wouldn't give a car or truck to a toddler to drive. Why are we thinking it's perfectly okay to give a device that the World Health Organization has said is a *possible human carcinogen*' to infants and toddlers, and for that matter, schoolchildren?"

Geena Davis

"My daughter was a toddler. I had no idea there was anything wrong with kids' media. I started watching little preschool shows with her or G-rated videos or whatever; I couldn't believe what I was seeing, that there seemed to be far more male characters than female characters in what we make for little kids. It was just a shock."

—

Sofia Coppola

"Having a kid, it makes you slow down; when you're walking with a toddler to pick up a leaf it can take a half-hour. You've never spent that time looking at a leaf before, having that kind of interaction. So, I think it does make you change the way you look at things."

—

Polly Berrien Berends

"Once we begin to appreciate that the apparent destructiveness of the toddler in taking apart a flower or knocking down sandcastles is, in fact, a constructive effort to understand unity, we are able to revise our view of the situation, moving from reprimand and prohibition to the intelligent channeling of his efforts and the fostering of discovery."

—

Jane Brody

"Dr. [Paula] Menyuk and her co-workers [at Boston University's School of Education] found that parents who supplied babies with a steady stream of information were not necessarily helpful. Rather, early, rich language skills were more likely to develop when parents provided lots of opportunities for their infants and toddlers to 'talk' and when parents listened and responded to the babies' communications."

—

Wendy Starland

"I first got interested in music as a toddler by my childhood babysitter, Rosetta Atkins. She taught me how to sing by imitating the voices on the gospel radio station she listened to - both men and women's voices."

—

Zooey Deschanel

"I grew up believing my sister was from the planet Neptune and had been sent down to Earth to kill me. I believed this because my sister Emily convinced me of it when I was a toddler. I think she'd seen Invasion of the Body Snatchers and her imagination ran away with her. There's a part of me that still believes it."

Robert Breault

"In a houseful of toddlers and pets, you can start out having a bad day, but you keep getting detoured."

P. J. O'Rourke

"For toddlers, I suggest leaving their mittens on year-round, indoors and out. That way they can't get into aspirin bottles, liquor cabinets, or boxes of kitchen matches."

J. J. Abrams

"Whenever a toddler sees a pile of blocks, he wants to tear it down."

Ricky Martin

"A lot of people say, 'Wow, you're a single father of twin boys, that's crazy!' Two toddlers can get hectic, but I wouldn't change it for anything.

Every day they teach me different things. The love is there. When you have a two-year-old saying every other hour, 'Papi, te amo. Papi, I love you,' it can't get better."

—

Elizabeth Gilbert

"Every try to take a toy away from a toddler? They don't like that, do they? They start kicking and screaming. Best way to take a toy away from a toddler is distract the kid, give him something else to play with. Instead of trying to forcefully take thoughts out of your mind, give your mind something better to play with."

—

John Green

"The sun was a toddler insistently refusing to go to bed: It was past eight-thirty and still light."

—

George Carlin

"When I ask how old your toddler is, I don't need to hear '27 months.' 'He's two' will do just fine.

He's not a cheese. And I didn't really care in the first place."

—

Jodi Picoult

"In my previous life, I was a civil attorney. At one point I truly believed that was what I wanted to be- but that was before I'd been handed a fistful of crushed violets from a toddler. Before I understood that the smile of a child is a tattoo: indelible art."

—

Voldane Pelt

I have no idea how accurate the numbers are on this next quote, but toddlers heal from everything at the speed of light and as we get older, we heal slower. Maybe the laughter is why we slow down our healing.

—

Joel Osteen

"Isn't it funny how babies laugh a lot? I read a toddler; a young child laughs 300 times a day. The average adult laughs, like, four times a day.

God put it in them. He put the laugh in us, but I think sometimes we let life get us down, you know, have bad breaks, and we lose our breaks."

—

Jon Ronson

"Of course, there are people who would like to eat breakfast without the screams of toddlers all around them, but those people should get over themselves and stop being stuck up and idiotic."

—

Phyllis Schlafly

"No country in history ever sent mothers of toddlers off to fight enemy soldiers until the United States did this in the Iraq war."

—

Jim Gaffigan

"Nursery schools and bars at 2 a.m. are the only places where it is completely normal if someone just spontaneously throws up on the floor...and just like a toddler, the bar patron wakes up the next day not remembering or caring how they behaved."

—

Barry Lane

"Time to a writer is like play dough in the hands of a toddler."

—

Tom Hodgkinson

"Computers tend to separate us from each other - Mum's on the laptop, Dad's on the iPad, teenagers are on Facebook, toddlers are on the DS, and so on."

—

Penelope Leach

"Grown-up people do very little and say a great deal... Toddlers say very little and do a great deal... With a toddler you cannot explain, you have to show. You cannot send, you have to take. You cannot control with words; you have to use your body.

—

Voldanc Pclt

I think they sense what she is speaking about in this next quote and that is why they want the cell phone.

—

Emily Yoffe

"Love is not shown by giving your toddler a car. It's better demonstrated by clapping as she bangs on pots or singing to her while she plays with her cheap little bath toys in the tub."

—

Jasper Fforde

"You speak baby gibberish?' asked Jack.

'Fluently. The adult-education center ran a course, and I have a lot of time on my hands.'

'So, what did he say?'

'I don't know.'

'I thought you said you spoke gibberish?'

'I do. But your baby doesn't. I think he's speaking either pre-toddler nonsense, a form of in fact burble or an obscure dialect of gobbledygook. In any event, I can't understand a word he's saying.'

'Oh."

James Dobson

"Tell me why it is that a toddler will gag over a perfectly wonderful breakfast of ham, eggs, biscuits, juice, and jelly. But then he will enthusiastically drink the dog's water and play in the toilet. Truly, he is his mother's greatest challenge...; and her most inexpressible joy."

Anne Lamott

"Toddlers can make you feel as if you have violated some archaic law in their personal Koran and you should die, infidel."

Mary Blakely

"In the range of things toddlers have to learn and endlessly review--why you can't put bottles with certain labels in your mouth, why you have to sit on the potty, why you can't take whatever you want in the store, why you don't hit your friends-- by the time we got to why you can't drop your peas, well, I was dropping a few myself."

Stanley Greenspan

"Even if you find yourself in a heated exchange with your toddler, it is better for your child to feel the heat rather than for him to feel you withdraw emotionally… Active and emotional involvement between parent and child helps the child make the limits a part of himself."

Nicole Polizzi

"I learned that buying expensive furniture with toddlers around is pointless."

Paul Bloom

"Families survive the terrible twos because toddlers aren't strong enough to kill with their hands and aren't capable of using lethal weapons."

Steven Pinker

"The stirrings of morality emerge early in childhood. Toddlers spontaneously offer toys and help to others and try to comfort people they see in distress."

—

Mariella Frostrup

"It's perfectly possible to love your toddler but struggle to like them when times are hard."

—

Jackie Chan

"The kids never listen to you, especially the youngest ones."

—

Tom Aikens

"Kids are very visual, and they might not eat a food just because of its colour."

—

H. Jackson Brown, Jr.

"Always kiss your children goodnight even if they're already asleep."

—

Nia Vardalos

"There are benefits to adopting a toddler. They can tell you what's wrong. And everything we did with our daughter was a first. Her first tooth fairy. Santa"

—

Beth Ann Fennelly

"With toddlers around, times are always interesting."

—

Hayden Thorne

"I'm sure the other kids wouldn't mind not being lectured by another toddler over the virtues of sharing and the mental benefits of toy blocks."

—

William Stafford

"Kids: they dance before they learn there is anything that isn't music."

—

Louise J. Kaplan

"The toddler must say no in order to find out who she is. The adolescent says no to assert who she is not."

—

Dorothy Corkille Briggs

"The toddler craves independence, but he fears desertion."

—

Ed Howe

"Families with babies and families without are so sorry for each other."

—

Lawrence Kutner

"The fundamental job of a toddler is to rule the universe."

Denis Leary

"Racism isn't born, folks, it's taught. I have a two-year-old son. You know what he hates? Naps! End of list."

—

Jerry Seinfeld

"A two-year-old is kind of like having a blender, but you don't have a top for it."

—

Anthony Bourdain

"If you've ever hauled a 28-pound two-year-old around New York, you'll find that men fold at the knees a lot quicker than women."

—

Erma Bombeck

"Why would anyone steal a shopping cart? It's like stealing a two-year-old."

—

Will Ferrell

"If you're flying with your children, it's best to book them on the same flight and not on one where they have more legroom and are leaving at a different time. They could get there earlier than you, and that causes resentment. Two-year-olds can also never figure out those connecting flights. It just makes it harder, so travel as a family."

—

Fred Rogers

"Parents find many different ways to work their way through the assertiveness of their two year-olds, but seeing that assertiveness as positive energy being directed toward growth as a competent individual may open up some new possibilities."

—

Glen Campbell

"I don't remember not singing. I started when I was, I don't know how - what, two years old, or a year old or something like that."

—

Mary Blakely

"One year, I'd completely lost my bearings trying to follow potty training instruction from a psychiatric expert. I was stuck on step on which stated without an atom of irony: "Before you begin, remove all stubbornness from the child.". . . I knew it only could have been written by someone whose suit coat was still spotless at the end of the day, not someone who had any hands-on experience with an actual two-year-old."

—

Ice Cube

"My son Darrel could recite 'Straight Outta Compton' at two years old. He loved it! You can expose your kids to anything as long as you sit there and explain it to them."

—

Tim Kinsella

"I was two years old when I told my mom I was going to be in a band when I grew up, and I was four years old when I started my first band with my neighbors. Before I knew how to do anything, I was figuring out how to be in a band.

—

Kristen Taekman

"My kids! They run so hot and cold. One minute, I am in complete control and feeling like Supermom, then the next minute, my two-year-old is having a tantrum in line at the supermarket and is inconsolable, and I feel so helpless and I want to crawl in a hole."

—

Janine and The Mixtape

"I got into music because my Dad used to tell everyone I had the voice of an angel when I was two years old."

—

David Walton

"A lot of people talk to kids like they're idiots. When I'm telling my two-year-old that you don't throw a dish on the floor, I explain it as if they're a 25-year-old that hasn't quite figured it out yet."

—

Voldane Pelt

You never know what a toddler will remember, or when.

—

Boris Kodjoe

"In Vienna, when I was a year-and-a-half or two-years-old. I remember it because I remember the little blue raincoat I used to wear, and how the buttons felt. I liked to walk on the street in front of our house when it was raining, and jump into all the puddles. That's weird, but that's my earliest memory."

—

Rodney Atkins

"I have a two-year-old. Just turned two a couple weeks ago, and he is my main man, he is my shadow. Every spare second, I am hanging with him."

—

Ray Romano

"You might think that's an exaggeration but believe me, if you leave twin two-year-olds alone in your living room, at some point a cow will be airborne."

—

Dan Stevens

"The female attention I have to struggle hardest with is from my two-year-old daughter."

—

Bernard Williams

"No symphony orchestra ever played music like a two-year-old girl laughing with a puppy."

—

Ray Romano

"I wasn't really that informed about the two-year-old. Oh, I'd read about them, and occasionally I'd see documentaries on the Discovery Channel showing two-year-olds in the wild, where they belong."

—

Josette Sheeran

"If a child in its first thousand days - from conception to two years old - does not have adequate nutrition, the damage is irreversible."

—

Orson Welles

"I know people who have a much better recollection of their childhood than I do. They remember very well when they were a year and a half and two years old. I've only one or two daguerreotypes that come to mind."

—

Vera Farmiga

"I have a two-year-old who just turned three, and my four-year-old just turned five. I have the same irrational feelings taking them to pre-school. It's this charged combination of stress and joy and anxiety and excitement. When they're away, you've got a sudden loss of purpose and this ever-present fear about the kid's welfare. The departure of our children from our nest is not an easy thing."

—

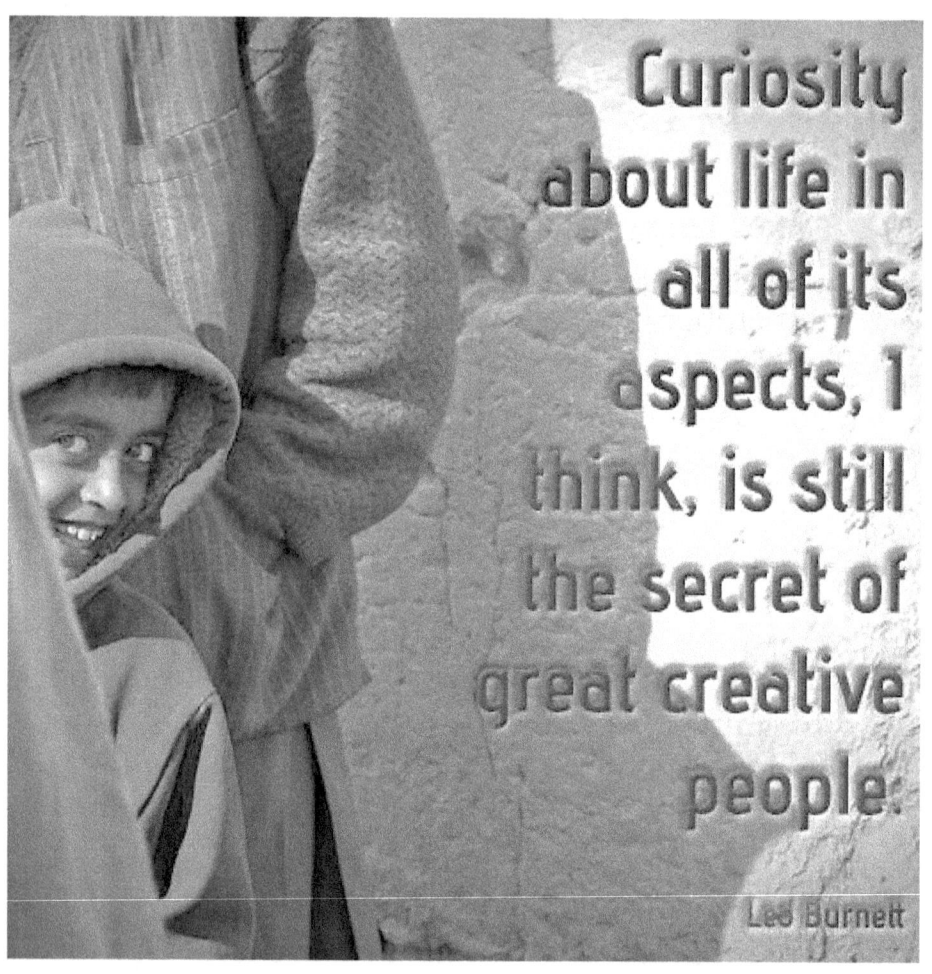

Seth MacFarlane

"I was about two years old when I first started drawing recognizable characters."

—

Aly Raisman

"I was two years old when my mom put me in mommy and me classes. I always had a lot of energy, so it was the perfect fit!"

—

Twyla Tharp

"What I do remember is visualization of the sound of music, seeing bodies in movement in relation to how music sounded, because my mother practiced at the keyboard a lot and I also went to her lessons. As a two-year-old, three-year-old I remember seeing things in movement."

—

Temple Grandin

"If you have a 2 or 3 year-old who is not talking, you must start an early intervention program.

The worst thing you can do with an autistic 3 year-old is to do nothing."

—

Patrick Dempsey

"One day my 3-year-old daughter said, 'Your very handsome, Poppy.' That was the best compliment ever."

—

Mark Hart

"I'm at my 3 years old's year-end concert. It's full of very off-key, mostly unfocused children, but this father is still beaming. Must be how God feels on Sunday."

—

Joaquin Phoenix

"I was 3 years old - to this day it is a vivid memory. My family and I were on a boat, catching fish. As one fish was caught, he was writhing, then he was thrown against the side of the boat. You couldn't disguise what it was. This was what we did to animals to eat them. The animal went from a living, vibrant creature fighting for life to a violent death. I recognized it, as did my brothers and sisters."

—

Daniel Clowes

"I must have been 3 years old or less, and I remember paging through these comics, trying to figure out the stories. I couldn't read the words, so I made up my own stories."

—

Rodney Dangerfield

"When I was 3 years old, my parents got a dog. I was jealous of the dog, so they got rid of me."

—

Elena Anaya

"I remember saying to my mom, 3 years old, every day, 'I can fly!' Living on the ninth floor, it was dangerous."

—

Ayelet Waldman

"There is an inverse correlation between the cleanliness of a bathroom and my 3-year-old daughter's need to move her bowels."

—

Kanye West

"I just close my eyes and act like I'm a 3 year old. I try to get as close to a childlike level as possible because we were all artists back then. So, you just close your eyes and think back to when you were as young as you can remember and had the least barriers to your creativity."

—

Teenagers

Preteen, teenagers, and young adults what gambit they run! The scary thing is that you will find a 13 year-old more mature than you will an 18 year-old and vice versa. You can truly not judge this age range based on only their years on earth.

They can be unruly or saints and often both in the same day. Somehow in my mind, we have toddlers as the transition to children from babies and teenagers are the rebellion of children to growing up.

The irony is that the teenager claims to only want to grow up.

Voldane Pelt

Mignon McLaughlin

"What a shame that allowances have to stop with the teens: both those that are paid to us and those that are made for us."

—

Johnny Depp

"As a teenager, I was so insecure. I was the type of guy that never fitted in because he never dared to choose. I was convinced I had absolutely no talent at all. For nothing. And that thought took away all my ambition, too."

—

Ellen DeGeneres

"Being a teenager and figuring out who you are is hard enough without someone attacking you."

—

Torbjorn Tannsjo

"When I was in my late teens I was already interested in philosophy."

—

D. H. Lawrence

"Oh, the innocent girl in her maiden teens knows perfectly well what everything means."

—

Dean Kamen

"You have teenagers thinking they're going to make millions as NBA stars when that's not realistic for even 1 percent of them. Becoming a scientist or engineer is."

—

Sophie Nelisse

"There are many animation films out there for teens, tweens, and family but there are not that many real-life stories."

—

Amy Astley

"A short way into Teen Vogue I realized that teens see it as a guide for their lives and their careers, more than a place to teach them how to get boys. And they don't ask us fashion advice questions; they're too sophisticated. They're inspired by what they see, and they think, 'These people at this magazine represent what I want to be, beyond shoes and makeup.'"

—

LeCrae

"In your late teens and early twenties, everything is idealism. Everything should just work in black and white. That's good. You need that. I think most revolutions are started by people in their teens and twenties."

—

David Levithan

"Teens wanted things that were real, that they connected with, it doesn't have to reflect reality directly. They love 'The Hunger Games' not because it's real in that it happens, but the emotions there are real, and it's very relatable."

—

Marilyn vos Savant

"I would not encourage children or teens to multitask because we don't know where those efforts may lead."

—

Joan Chen

"All teenagers have this desire to somehow run away."

—

Meg Cabot

"I actually love writing for teens best. I had such an awful time in my own teen years - I love having the chance to relive them through my fiction."

—

Dave Barry

"Your modern teenager is not about to listen to advice from an old person, defined as a person who remembers when there was no Velcro."

—

Ezra Taft Benson

"Too often the pressure for popularity, on children and teens, places an economic burden on the income of the father, so mother feels she must go to work to satisfy her children's needs. That decision can be most shortsighted."

—

Renee Watson

"For me, the lives of children and teens are interesting - they are always changing. There's just so much to sort through. All of this makes for good plots and complex characters."

—

Ariana Grande

"I can't stress to you enough how much I can relate to teens being cyberbullied. Something that helps me is looking at old videos of me and my friends from middle school or videos of my family. I love watching funny videos of my favorite people - it really cheers me up."

—

Linda Fiorentino

"Teens aren't just interested in getting laid. I won't believe that's all they're interested in. I have four younger sisters and they're sick of being shown how they're supposed to react in bed."

—

Jeff Allen

"I believe teenagers are God's revenge on mankind. It's like He said, 'Hey let's see how they like it to create something in their own image that denies their existence.'"

—

Markus Zusak

"We underestimate teenagers at our peril. Even the dismissive thing out on the street--look at what they're wearing. Then we'll hear stories about how a toddler fell on the tracks, and it's often a teenager who comes to the rescue and walks away because he or she doesn't want any credit. I recognize it because I've written books for teenagers--it's basically that they feel things more than adults do. They want things more than you think. They want things with greater depth than you think they do. Teenagers have got a lot of soul, that adults have forgotten they have within themselves."

—

John Knowles

"Teenagers today are more free to be themselves and to accept themselves."

—

Alfonso Cuaron

"I find it very stupid that teenagers could only see caricatures of teenagers, but they couldn't see films that you try to be a truthful context, a truthful portrayal of teenagers."

—

George Stults

"All I wanted to do while I was a teenager was go out and play most of the time and just enjoy life and have fun. I wasn't big into school, you know, I look back now and wish I would have spent more time studying and enjoyed it more. It's not for everyone and I didn't enjoy it that much like going to school and studying - some stuff I did but some of it I didn't. My attention span wasn't there."

—

Quotes for Parents

Brian K. Vaughan

"I genuinely am sort of an emotionally stunted man-child, so if I just write to the top of my intelligence, it sounds like a teenager. I like being around teenagers. It's good for drama; they feel everything much more intensely than adults do; their lives are much more interesting than ours. They're mutants. They have these weird bodies that are rebelling against them and changing every day. Teenagers always equal good drama."

—

Unknown

"Drama, lies, tears...teenage years."

—

Elizabeth Gillies

"I love being a teen because you don't have all the responsibilities of an adult yet."

—

Fran Lebowitz

"As a teenager, you are at the last stage in your life when you will be happy to hear that the phone is for you."

Marilyn vos Savant

"Teens think listening to music helps them concentrate. It doesn't. It relieves them of the boredom that concentration on homework induces."

Jonathan Lethem

"Teenage life - possibly adult life too is all about what you want and can't have. And then about what you receive and misuse."

Hayley Williams

"No boy is worth your teenage years!"

Aimee Teegarden

"The teenage years are ridiculously crucial and hard and, um, awkward."

Logan Pearsall Smith

"Don't laugh at a youth for his affectations; he is only trying on one face after another to find a face of his own."

—

Aristotle

"Young people are in a condition like permanent intoxication, because youth is sweet, and they are growing."

—

Amity Shlaes

"The donning of the earbuds marks the beginning of teen life when children set off on their own for the passage through adolescence."

—

Quentin Crisp

"The young always have the same problem how to rebel and conform at the same time. They have now solved this by defying their parents and copying" one another.

Robert Brault

"In the time it takes you to understand a 14-year-old, he turns 15."

Unknown

"It's difficult to decide whether growing pains are something teenagers have or are."

Beverly Mitchell

"I think the hardest part about being a teenager is dealing with other teenagers - the criticism and the ridicule, the gossip, and rumors."

Ben Weasel

"I haven't really forgotten what it's like to be a teenager and how much it sucked."

Unknown

"A teenager is always too tired to hold a dishcloth, but never too tired to hold a phone."

—,

Rick Springfield

"I was a happy kid up until I hit the teen years."

—

Halsey

"When you're a teenage girl, a lot of being pretty has to do with your hair." —

Diane Lane

"Sometimes I think opposable thumbs were invented so teenage girls could use text messaging."

—

Michael J. Saylor

"Whenever teenage girls and corporate CEOs covet the same new technology, something extraordinary is happening."

Jessamyn West

"At fourteen you don't need sickness or death for tragedy."

Orlando Bloom

"A friend told me that teenage girls are always looking for someone to pin their dreams on. That doesn't make it any less weird though."

Lindsey Stirling

"There are very few things that I love more than being on stage and performing, but more than anything, I want to be a positive role model for teenage girls."

Brando Skyhorse

"The time between your first major fight with your best friend until you make up is, for a teenage girl, about as long as it took for God to create the universe. . ... It's excellent training for having a boyfriend."

—

Rob Thomas

"Teenage years are hard. And, having taught high school for a number of years, I think they're particularly hard on teenage girls. The most self-conscious human beings on the planet are teenage girls."

—

Tara Lynne Barr

"Teenage girls in television and film, in my experience, oftentimes are portrayed as either the sweet, innocent virgin or the super-sexy, experienced, town bicycle. There never seems to be an in-between. I think most girls are somewhere in between those two tropes."

—

Candice Olson

"Things have changed a lot since the earth was cooling and I was a teenage girl, but the basics of teenage bedrooms have remained the same.

Every girl wants a place that they are proud to call their own and where they can express their own individuality."

—

Raymond Duncan

"The best substitute for experience is being sixteen."

—

Alexandra Adornetto

"We teenage girls are faced with a quandary: we know what we want but are forced to wait for our male counterparts to grow up. We are ready for intense and meaningful relationships, but research indicates that males will not reach maturity until their mid-20s."

—

Candice Olson

"Ask any teenage girl to describe her perfect bedroom, and you'll get answers like 'a room with a private phone line, a place to hang out with friends, and for it to be way-cool and funky.' Ask parents the same question, and 'a locked door that opens on their 21st birthday' might top the list!"

—

Nora Ephron

"When your children are teenagers, it's important to have a dog so that someone in the house is happy to see you."

—

Vanessa Bayer

"There are just so many funny kids and teenagers. They're just not aware of how funny they are."

—

Art Buchwald

"It was a dangerous profession I had chosen ... because no one likes a funny kid. In fact, adults are scared silly of them and tend to warn children who act out that they are going to wind up in prison or worse. It is only when you grow up that they pay you vast sums of money to make them laugh."

—

Jamie Lee Curtis

"Well, I could do it for a day, but I wouldn't want to be a teenager again. I really wouldn't."

—

Doug Larson

"Few things are more satisfying than seeing your own children have teenagers of their own."

—

E. W. Howe

"It is hard to convince a high-school student that he will encounter a lot of problems more difficult than those of algebra and geometry."

—

Jamie Lee Curtis

"If you just watch a teenager, you see a lot of uncertainty."

—

Erma Bombeck

"Never lend your car to anyone to whom you have given birth."

—

Sophia Bush

"Being a teenager is an amazing time and a hard time. It's when you make your best friends - I have girls who will never leave my heart and I still talk to. You get the best and the worst as a teen. You have the best friendships and the worst heartbreaks."

—

Jaden Smith

"Kids who go to normal school are so teenagery, so angsty."

—

Justin Timberlake

"My teenage years were exactly what they were supposed to be. Everybody has their own path. It's laid out for you. It's just up to you to walk it."

—

Edgar Friedenberg

"The teenager seems to have replaced the Communist as the appropriate target for public controversy and foreboding."

—

Jena Malone

"Adolescence isn't just about prom or wearing sparkly dresses."

—

Judith Martin

"The invention of the teenager was a mistake. Once you identify a period of life in which people get to stay out late but don't have to pay taxes - naturally, no one wants to live any other way."

—

Rowan Blanchard

"Teenagers have a legitimate voice. We deserve to have a seat at the table and a place in the conversation. We're not exempt from politics and social movements; we're affected by them."

—

Art Buchwald

"There isn't a child who hasn't gone out into the brave new world who eventually doesn't return to the old homestead carrying a bundle of dirty clothes."

—

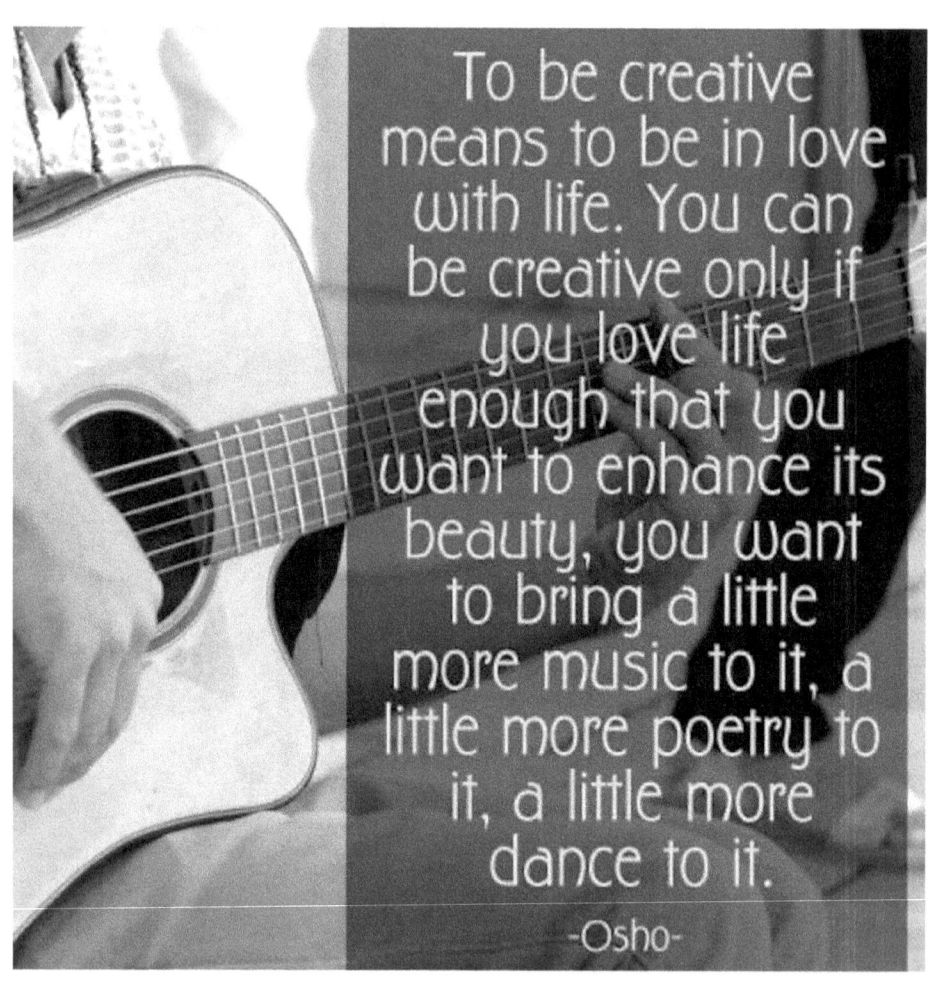

Pulling Hair, At the end of the Rope, Inspirational

As wonderful as being a parent is sometimes it's nice to have some inspiration to face the next catastrophe while waiting on their next miracle. This chapter there are quotes to inspire and while most are aimed at parents some are just inspiring and thrown in because parents are more than the sum of their kids.

Even if sometimes it doesn't feel like it. And last, in this section, you will find some quotes with no purpose beyond making you smile. Because smiling is half the job of parenting.

Voldane Pelt

"I have not failed.
I've just found 10,000
ways that won't work."
— Thomas A. Edison

Mitch Albom

"When you look into your mother's eyes, you know that is the purest love you can find on this earth."

—

J. K. Rowling

Love as powerful as your mother's, for you leaves its own mark to have been loved so deeply … will give us some protection forever.

—

Sue Atkins

"There is no such thing as a perfect parent. So just be a real one."

—

Sophie Kinsella

"There's nothing like your mother's sympathetic voice to make you want to burst into tears."

—

Abraham Lincoln

"All that I am, or hope to be, I owe to my mother."

—

Ewan McGregor

"The thing about parenting rules is there aren't any. That's what makes it so difficult."

—

Jodi Picoult

"Parents aren't the people you come from. They're the people you want to be when you grow up."

—

Unknown

"A father's goodness is higher than the mountain, a mother's goodness deeper than the sea."

—

Dr. T. P. Chia

"A good father is a source of inspiration and self-restraint. A good mother is the root of kindness and humbleness."

—

Shinichi Suzuki

"Children learn to smile from their parents."

—

Rick Riordan

"Have you ever noticed how parents can go from the most wonderful people in the world to totally embarrassing in three seconds?"

—

Susan Sarandon

"I just want my kids to love who they are, have happy lives

and find something they want to do and make peace with that.

Your job as a parent is to give your kids not only the instincts and talents to survive, but help them enjoy their lives."

—

Azriel Johnson

"Stepparents are not around to replace a biological parent, rather augment a child's life experience."

—

Matthew Jacobson

" Behind every young child who believes in himself is a parent who believed first."

—

Jim Carrey

"I got a lot of support from my parents. That's the one thing I always appreciated. They didn't tell me I was being stupid; they told me I was being funny."

—

Chrissy Teigen

"My biggest parenting conundrum why is it so hard to put someone who is already sleepy to sleep."

—

Charles R. Swindoll

"Each day of our lives we make deposits in the memory banks of our children."

—

William Attwood

"Don't demand respect as a parent. Demand civility and insist on honesty.

But respect is something you must earn-with kids as well as with adults."

—

Rose Kennedy

"I looked on childrearing not only as a work of love and duty, but as a profession that was fully interesting and challenging as any honorable profession in the world, and one that demanded the best that I could bring to it."

—

Gary Smalley

"Affirming words from moms and dads are like light switches.

Speak a word of affirmation at the right moment in a child's life

and it's like lighting up a whole roomful of possibilities."

—

Elizabeth Stone

"Making the decision to have a child is momentous. It is to decide forever

to have your heart go walking around outside your body."

—

Benjamin Spock

"The child supplies the power, but the parents have to do the steering."

—

Japanese Proverb

"When you have children yourself, you begin to understand what you owe your parents."

—

Quotes for Parents

Unknown

"The problem with being a parent is that by the time you are experienced, you are usually unemployed."

—

Hain Ginott

"The world talks to the mind. Parents speak more intimately; they talk to the heart."

—

Peter de Vries

"There are times when parenthood seems nothing but feeding the mouth that bites you."

—

Henry Ward Beecher

"There is no friendship, no love, like that of the parent for the child."

—

Kahlil Gibran

"You are the bows from which your children as living arrows are sent forth."

—

Richard L. Evans

"Children will not remember you for the material things you provided but for the feeling that you cherished them."

—

Voldane Pelt

"This one is really important in today's world."

—

Rachel Carson

"If a child is to keep alive his inborn sense of wonder, he needs the companionship of at least one adult who can share it, rediscovering with him the joy, excitement, and mystery of the world we live in."

—

Joyce Maynard

"It's not only children who grow. Parents do too. As much as we watch to see what our children do with their lives, they are watching us, to see what we do with ours. I can't tell my children to reach for the sun. All I can do is reach for it, myself."

—

Debra Ginsberg

"Through the blur, I wondered if I was alone or if other parents felt the same way I did - that everything involving our children was painful in some way. The emotions, whether they were joy, sorrow, love or pride, were so deep and sharp that in the end they left you raw, exposed and yes, in pain. The human heart was not designed to beat outside the human body and yet, each child represented just that - a parent's heart bared, beating forever outside its chest."

—

Nicholas Sparks

"What it's like to be a parent: It's one of the hardest things you'll ever do but in exchange, it teaches you the meaning of unconditional love."

Anne Frank

"Parents can only give good advice or put them on the right paths, but the final forming of a person's character lies in their own hands."

Frank A. Clark

"A baby is born with a need to be loved - and never outgrows it."

Wilson Mizner

"What feeling is so nice as a child's hand in yours? So small, so soft and warm, like a kitten huddling in the shelter of your clasp."

Thomas Bray

"Never fear spoiling children by making them too happy. Happiness is the atmosphere in which all good affections grow"

Jodi Picoul

"I think once you sign on to be a mother, that's the only shift they offer."

t—

P. J. O'Rourke

"Everybody knows how to raise children, except the people who have them."

—

Robert Breault

"It is one thing to show your child the way, and a harder thing to then stand out of it"

—

Jill Churchill

"There is no way to be a perfect mother and a million ways to be a good one."

—

William Shakespeare

"The voice of parents is the voice of gods, for to their children they are heaven's lieutenants."

—

Peter Krause

"Parenthood...It's about guiding the next generation and forgiving the last."

—

Garrison Keillor

"Nothing you do for children is ever wasted."

—

Carl Jung

"If there is anything that we wish to change in the child, we should first examine it and see whether it is not something that could better be changed in ourselves."

—

Carl Jung

"Nothing has a stronger influence psychologically on their environment and especially on their children than the unlived life of the parent."

—

Carl Jung

"I feel very strongly that I am under the influence of things or questions which were left incomplete and unanswered by my parents and grandparents and more distant ancestors. It often seems as if there were an impersonal karma within a family which is passed on from parents to children. It has always seemed to me that I had to answer questions which fate had posed to my forefathers, and which had not yet been answered, or as if I had to complete, or perhaps continue, things which previous ages had left unfinished."

—

Virginia Satir

"Every word, facial expression, gesture, or action on the part of a parent gives the child some message about self-worth. It is sad that so many parents don't realize what messages they are sending."

—

BEST RELATIONSHIP: TALK LIKE BESTFRIENDS, PLAY LIKE CHILDREN, ARGUE LIKE HUSBAND AND WIFE, PROTECT EACH OTHER LIKE BROTHER AND SISTER.

Virginia Satir

"Parents teach in the toughest school in the world - The School for Making People. You are the **board of education, the principal, the classroom teacher, and the janitor.**"

—

Virginia Satir

"It's sad that children cannot know their parents when they were younger; when they were loving, courting, and being nice to one another. By the time children are old enough to observe, the romance has all too often faded or gone underground."

—

Nelson Mandela

"Few things make the life of a parent more rewarding and sweet as successful children."

—

Buddy Hackett

"As a child my family's menu consisted of two choices: take it or leave it."

—

Jean Kerr

"The real menace in dealing with a five-year-old is that in no time at all you begin to sound like a five-year-old."

—

Barbara Kingsolver

"It kills you to see them grow up. But I guess it would kill you quicker if they didn't."

—

Sam Levenson

"Insanity is hereditary; you get it from your children."

—

Mark Twain

"When I was a boy of 14, my father was so ignorant I could hardly stand to have the old man around. But when I got to be 21, I was astonished at how much the old man had learned in seven years."

—

Ed Asner

"Raising kids is part joy and part guerrilla warfare."

—

Mark Twain

"Children are natural mimics who act like their parents despite every effort to teach them good manners."

—

King Edward VIII

"The thing that impresses me most about America is the way parents obey their children."

—

Erma Bombeck

"All of us have moments in our lives that test our courage. Taking children into a house with a white carpet is one of them."

—

Phyllis Diller

"Most children threaten at times to run away from home. This is the only thing that keeps some parents going."

—

Mignon McLaughlin

"A parent who has never apologized to his children is a monster. If he's always apologizing, his children are monsters."

—

Karen Brown

"My mom used to say it doesn't matter how many kids you have… because one kid'll take up 100% of your time so more kids can't possibly take up more than 100% of your time."

—

BE STRONG
but not rude
BE KIND
but not weak
BE BOLD
but not bully
BE HUMBLE
but not timid
BE PROUD
but not arrogant

Steve Martin

"A father carries pictures where his money used to be."

—

Jim Gaffigan

"There should be a children's song: 'If you're happy and you know it, keep it to yourself and let your dad sleep'."

—

P. J. O'Rourke

"Getting down on all fours and imitating a rhinoceros stops babies from crying. (Put an empty cigarette pack on your nose for a horn and make loud "snort" noises.) I don't know why parents don't do this more often. Usually, it makes the kid laugh. Sometimes it sends him into shock. Either way, it quiets him down. If you're a parent, acting like a rhino has another advantage. Keep it up until the kid is a teenager and he definitely won't have his friends hanging around your house all the time."

—

Mignon McLaughlin

"Ma-ma does everything for the baby, who responds by saying Da-da first."

—

Vicki Lansky

"You will always be your child's favorite toy."

—

Robert Breault

"Parenthood is the passing of a baton, followed by a lifelong disagreement as to who dropped it."

—

Haim Ginott

"Parents often talk about the younger generation as if they didn't have anything to do with it."

—

Woody Allen

"I don't think my parents liked me. They put a live teddy bear in my crib."

Phyllis Diller

"It would seem that something which means poverty, disorder and violence every single day should be avoided entirely, but the desire to beget children is a natural urge."

Michelle Pfeiffer

"Like all parents, my husband and I just do the best we can, hold our breath and hope we've set aside enough money for our kid's therapy."

Sydney J. Harris

"The beauty of 'spacing' children many years apart lies in the fact that parents have time to learn the mistakes that were made with the older ones - which permits them to make exactly the opposite mistakes with the younger ones."

William Feather

"Setting a good example for your children takes all the fun out of middle age."

—

Phyllis Diller

"We spend the first twelve months of our children's lives teaching them to walk and talk and the next twelve telling them to sit down and shut up."

—

Homer

"It behooves a father to be blameless if he expects his child to be."

—

Calvin Trillin

"The most remarkable thing about my mother is that for thirty years she served the family nothing but leftovers. The original meal has never been found."

—

P. J. O'Rourke

"Humans are the only animals that have children on purpose with the exception of guppies, who like to eat theirs."

—

Phyllis Diller

"Always be nice to your children because they are the ones who will choose your rest home."

—

Phyllis Diller

"I want my children to have all the things I couldn't afford. Then I want to move in with them."

—

Sydney J. Harris

"When I hear somebody sigh, 'Life is hard,' I am always tempted to ask, 'Compared to what?'"

—

Ashleigh Brilliant

"For some strange reason, no matter where I go, the place is always called 'here'."

—

Ozzy Osbourne

"Of all the things I've lost, I miss my mind the most."

—

Sherrilyn Kenyon

"Life isn't finding shelter in the storm. It's about learning to dance in the rain."

—

Napoleon Bonaparte

"Never interrupt your enemy when he is making a mistake."

—

Albert Schweitzer

"Success is not the key to happiness. Happiness is the key to success. If you love what you are doing, you will be successful."

Belva Davis

"Don't be afraid of the space between your dreams and reality. If you can dream it, you can make it so."

—

Rabindranath Tagore

"Everything comes to us that belongs to us if we create the capacity to receive it."

—

Jennifer Lopez

"Doubt is a killer. You just have to know who you are and what you stand for."

—

Winston Churchill

"Never give up on something that you can't go a day without thinking about."

—

Maya Angelou

"If you are always trying to be normal you will never know how amazing, you can be."

—

Stephen Covey

"I am not a product of my circumstances. I am a product of my decisions."

—

Socrates

"To find yourself, think for yourself."

—

Maya Angelou

"We delight in the beauty of the butterfly, but rarely admit the changes it has gone through to achieve that beauty."

—

Will Durant

"Forget mistakes. Forget failure. Forget everything except what you're going to do now and do it. Today is your lucky day"

—

Joseph Addison

"Three grand essentials to happiness in this life are something to do, something to love, and something to hope for."

—

Paulo Coelho

"Don't allow your wounds to transform you into someone you are not."

—

Hoda Kotb

"There are two types of people: The ones who give you 50 reasons it can't be done ... and the ones who just do it."

—

Theodore Roosevelt

"Believe you can and you're halfway there."

—

C. S. Lewis

"Getting over a painful experience is much like crossing monkey bars. You have to let go at some point in order to move forward."

—

Benjamin Franklin

"When you are good to others, you are best to yourself."

—

Susan Sontag

"Do stuff. be clenched, curious. Not waiting for inspiration's shove or society's kiss on your forehead. Pay attention. It's all about paying attention. attention is vitality. It connects you with others. It makes you eager. stay eager."

—

Henry David Thoreau

"If one advances confidently in the direction of his dreams, and endeavors to live the life which he has imagined, he will meet with a success unexpected in common hours."

—

Wayne Dyer

"Loving people live in a loving world. Hostile people live in a hostile world. Same world."

—

Chief Seattle

"Man does not weave this web of life. He is merely a strand of it. Whatever he does to the web, he does to himself."

—

Katharine Hepburn

"Life is hard. After all, it kills you."

—

Ralph Waldo Emerson

"The only person you are destined to become is the person you decide to be."

—

Walt Disney

"If you can dream it, you can do it."

—

Paulo Coelho

"It's the possibility of having a dream come true that makes life interesting."

—

Chuck Palahniuk

"Nothing of me is original. I am the combined effort of everyone I've ever known."

—

Steve Jobs

"That's been one of my mantras - focus and simplicity. Simple can be harder than complex: You have to work hard to get your thinking clean to make it simple. But it's worth it in the end because once you get there, you can move mountains."

—

Martin Luther King, Jr.

"Never succumb to the temptation of bitterness."

—

Ruby Dee

"The kind of beauty I want most is the hard-to-get kind that comes from within - strength, courage, dignity."

—

George Lucas

"No! Try not. Do, or do not. There is no try."

—

Alexander Graham Bell

"Concentrate all your thoughts upon the work at hand. The sun's rays do not burn until brought to a focus."

—

Joseph Addison

"It is only imperfection that complains of what is imperfect. The more perfect we are, the more gentle and quiet we become, towards the defects of others."

—

Ayn Rand

"The question isn't who is going to let me; it's who is going to stop me."

—

Elizabeth Gilbert

"Stop wearing your wishbone where your backbone ought to be."

—

Sherman Alexie

"If you let people into your life a little bit, they can be pretty damn amazing."

—

Mark Twain

"Keep away from people who try to belittle your ambitions. Small people always do that, but the really great make you feel that you, too, can become great."

—

Isaac Newton

"Nature is pleased with simplicity. And nature is no dummy."

—

Maya Angelou

"It's one of the greatest gifts you can give yourself, to forgive. Forgive everybody."

—

Les Brown

"Help others achieve their dreams and you will achieve yours."

—

Richard Branson

"If somebody offers you an amazing opportunity but you are not sure you can do it, say yes, then learn how to do it later!"

—

Elizabeth Taylor

"You just do it. You force yourself to get up. You force yourself to put one foot before the other, and God damn it, you refuse to let it get to you. You fight. You cry. You curse. Then you go about the business of living. That's how I've done it. There's no other way."

—

Dave Barry

"Never under any circumstances take a sleeping pill and a laxative on the same night."

—

Benny Hill

"Have you noticed that all the people in favor of birth control are already born?"

—

Emo Philips

"I asked God for a bike, but I know God doesn't work that way. So, I stole a bike and asked for forgiveness."

—

Charles Wadsworth

"By the time a man realizes that his father was right, he has a son who thinks he's wrong."

—

Isaac Asimov

"People who think they know everything are a great annoyance to those of us who do."

—

Walter Matthau

"My doctor gave me six months to live, but when I couldn't pay the bill, he gave me six months more."

—

George Carlin

"I went to a bookstore and asked the saleswoman, 'Where's the self-help section?' She said if she told me, it would defeat the purpose."

—

George Burns

"Happiness is having a large, loving, caring, close-knit family in another city."

—

Robert Bloch

"The man who smiles when things go wrong has thought of someone to blame it on."

—

Lily Tomlin

"Why is it that when we talk to God, we're said to be praying but when God talks to us, we're schizophrenic?"

—

Mark Twain

"Nothing spoils a good story like the arrival of an eyewitness."

—

Oscar Wilde

"Always borrow money from a pessimist. He won't expect it back."

—

Oscar Wilde

"Women are meant to be loved, not to be understood."

—

Agatha Christie

"An archaeologist is the best husband a woman can have. The older she gets the more interested he is in her."

—

Yogi Berra

"You should always go to other people's funerals, otherwise, they won't come to yours."

Will Rogers

"When I die, I want to die like my grandfather who died peacefully in his sleep. Not screaming like all the passengers in his car."

Jim Davis

"Avoid fruits and nuts. You are what you eat."

Ellen DeGeneres

"Accept who you are. Unless you're a serial killer."

Steven Wright

"I couldn't repair your brakes, so I made your horn louder."

Ann Brashares

"When you're about to criticize someone, walk a mile in their shoes, that way when you criticize them, you're a mile away from them and you have their shoes"

—

Jill Shalvis

"A conclusion is the place you get to when you're tired of thinking."

—

William S. Burroughs

"After one look at this planet, any visitor from outer space would say 'I want to see the manager.'"

—

Timothy Leary

"Women who seek to be equal with men lack ambition."

—

Benjamin Franklin

"Three may keep a secret if two of them are dead."

—

Rodney Dangerfield

"I haven't spoken to my wife in years. I didn't want to interrupt her."

—

Ann Landers

"Television has proved that people will look at anything rather than each other."

—

Milton Berle

"Committee - a group of men who keep minutes and waste hours."

—

Ronald Reagan

"It has been said that politics is the second oldest profession. I have learned that it bears a striking resemblance to the first."

—

Joan Rivers

"I hate housework! You make the beds; you do the dishes and six months later you have to start all over again."

—

P. J. O'Rourke

"There are a number of mechanical devices which increase sexual arousal, particularly in women. Chief among these is the Mercedes-Benz 380SL convertible."

—

Mark Twain

"Men are like bank accounts. The more money, the more interest they generate."

—

Bob Thaves

"Inside me, there's a thin person struggling to get out, but I can usually sedate him with four or five cupcakes."

—

Bob Hope

"I grew up with six brothers. That's how I learned to dance - waiting for the bathroom."

—

Steve Martin

"First, the doctor told me the good news: I was going to have a disease named after me."

—

Doug Larson

"Life expectancy would grow by leaps and bounds if green vegetables smelled as good as bacon."

—

James Thurber

"Well, if I called the wrong number, why did you answer the phone?"

Matt Groening

"English? Who needs that? I'm never going to England."

Natalie Wood

"The only time a woman really succeeds in changing a man is when he is a baby."

Henny Youngman

"If at first, you don't succeed... so much for skydiving."

Wendy Liebman

"My husband wanted one of those big-screen TVs for his birthday. So, I just moved his chair closer to the one we have already."

Lana Turner

"A successful man is one who makes more money than his wife can spend. A successful woman is one who can find such a man."

—

Ashleigh Brilliant

"To be sure of hitting the target, shoot first, and call whatever you hit the target."

—

Oscar Wilde

"Some cause happiness wherever they go; others, whenever they go."

—

Rodney Dangerfield

"I told my wife the truth. I told her I was seeing a psychiatrist. Then she told me the truth: that she was seeing a psychiatrist, two plumbers, and a bartender."

—

Quotes for Parents

Robert Bloch

"Friendship is like peeing on yourself: everyone can see it, but only you get the warm feeling that it brings."

—

Ronald Reagan

"It's true hard work never killed anybody, but I figure, why take the chance?"

—

Milton Berle

"The problem with life is, by the time you can read women like a book, your library card has expired."

—

Evan Esar

"The best time to give advice to your children is while they're still young enough to believe you know what you're talking about."

—

Jim Morrison

"I see myself as an intelligent, sensitive human, with the soul of a clown which forces me to blow it at the most important moments."

—

Les Dawson

"I used to sell furniture for a living. The trouble was, it was my own."

—

Bob Hope

"A bank is a place that will lend you money if you can prove that you don't need it."

—

George Carlin

"A house is just a place to keep your stuff while you go out and get more stuff."

—

Marilyn Monroe

"If you can make a girl laugh, you can make her do anything."

—

Kristen Schaal

"I think growing up on a farm in a certain amount of isolation, with not a lot of friends nearby, makes you entertain yourself and kind of grows your imagination - being alone is quite good for all that. You make up stories, talk to the animals, let them be an audience, a bunch of cows."

—

Erma Bombeck

"Do you know what you call those who use towels and never wash them, eat meals and never do the dishes, sit in rooms they never clean, and are entertained till they drop? If you have just answered, 'A house guest,' you're wrong because I have just described my kids."

—

Rodney Dangerfield

"What a childhood I had. My parents sent me to a child psychiatrist. The kid didn't help me at all."

—

Rodney Dangerfield

"With my old man I got no respect. He told me never take candy from a stranger unless he offered me a ride."

—

Sports & Music

Music and sports are two of the things that seem to become a series of trips, errands, expenses for the parents and still have a positive impact on children's lives. The crack of the bat or sound of chopsticks, when combined with your child, has an almost magical way of making them important.

The quotes in this chapter are music and sports-related and while not each one will say the word child, children or kid in the quote all we have to do is think about the quote as parents and we can feel how it relates to parents and children.

The next time your waiting in line for a uniform or for your child's team to finish showering and be ready to go home you can read a few of these and maybe that way will feel less onerous.

Voldane Pelt

Fred Frith

"Well, I think music for kids is never anything but experimental is it?"

—

Talib Kweli

"Young kids should be doing music that has shock value. They'll grow out of "it.

—

William Stafford

"Kids: they dance before they learn there is anything that isn't music."

—

Mayer Hawthorne

"I don't want kids listening to my music thinking it's for their parents. I want them to feel it's theirs."

—

Martin Gore

"All of my kids are into music. My older daughter plays guitar, piano, sings. My young son, he sings."

—

Didi Conn

"[Kids today] think "Grease" is just one long music video. So, they watch it over and over again the way we when we were kids, we listened to albums."

—

Ingrid Michaelson

"I think kids who have music in their lives are more focused. They have better attention spans. They excel more in their studies. They have a better sense of self-esteem and self-worth."

—

Ringo Starr

"The kids are interested in the music of them. They're not interested in mop-tops and Beatle boots and crazy suits. It's all down to the music now - that's what they hear, and that's what they love."

Erik Parker

"Hip hop has evolved, thankfully. Kids are making music that is important to their lives and outlooks."

—

Rod Stewart

"I have enough music coming out of my kids' bedrooms when I'm at home."

—

Juliana Hatfield

"The whole thing about rock music, pop music, is it's really for kids."

—

Lenny Kravitz

"I think kids in Europe have developed a deeper knowledge of music and of black music in particular. You go to Europe, and these kids know about all this obscure funk and soul that kids over here wouldn't know. I think it's getting better in the States, though, with the age of the Internet."

—

Andrew Hollander

"As a kid, I was always listening to music. I would just go into my room and put on an album, read the lyrics, and just spend hours and hours in there. Plus, my sister Laurie played piano (in fact she taught me my first few notes) so music was always around one way or another."

—

Dweezil Zappa

I" really want younger audience members to see kids in their early 20's playing Frank's music and to be inspired to take things to a higher level themselves."

—

Stephen Stills

"I got hooked into folk music by accident because that's what white college kids liked when I was a child"

—

Quincy Jones

"Hell, nobody knows where jazz is going to go. There may be a kid right now in Chitlin Switch, Georgia, who is going to come along and upset everybody."

—

James Bay

"I loved pop music as a little kid. Things like the Black Eyed Peas. If it had a catchy chorus, I was into it."

—

Carrie Brownstein

"As a kid, before I got into music, I did all the drama classes, went to theater camp in the summers, so it wasn't totally a foreign world."

—

Mark Lawrenson

"My iPod's unbelievable. Seriously. The kids have put most of the music on it but there's a complete mix of 80s rubbish and current day stuff."

Miles Teller

"My mom is very proud of introducing music to all her kids. But I played in some bad rock bands my junior and senior years of high school."

Jimi Hendrix

"I'm gonna put a curse on you and all your kids will be born completely naked."

Kurt Cobain

"I get a thrill meeting kids who are into alternative music."

Albert Einstein

"There exists a passion for comprehension, just as there exists a passion for music. That passion is rather common in children but gets lost in most people later on. Without this passion, there would be neither mathematics nor natural science."

—

Eddie Van Halen

"Music kept me off the streets and out of trouble and gave me something that was mine that no one could take away from me."

—

Eddie Van Halen

"If I can help a kid discover a liking or even a passion for music in their life, then that's a wonderful thing."

—

Sarah McLachlan

"I do think music and the arts are imperative for our kids for their creative learning and their emotional education, which breeds better adults. I'm doing what I can to try and pick up the slack and I applaud anyone who tries to give back to their community."

—

Horace Panter

"I still get a buzz from seeing young kids making music."

—

Tom Cochrane

"I even got letters from kids in hospitals saying the music is what keeps them going, and that really touched my heart."

—

Michael J. Fox

"As a kid, I was into music, played guitar in a band. Then I started acting in plays in junior high school and just got lost in the puzzle of acting, the magic of it. I think it was an escape for me."

—

Dustin Diamond

"Kids these days don't know as much about music as they think they do."

—

Quotes for Parents

Billy Higgins

"Because the stuff that they feed kids now, they'll have a bunch of idiots in the next millennium as far as art and culture is concerned."

—

Billy Higgins

"There's so much beautiful music in the world and the kids are getting robbed."

Billy Higgins

"I enjoy seeing young people being interested in what they can do."

—

Gerald R. Ford

"Music education opens doors that help children pass from school into the world around them - a world of work, culture, intellectual activity, and human involvement. The future of our nation depends on providing our children with a complete education that includes music."

—

Leonard Bernstein

"Children must receive music instruction as naturally as food, with as much pleasure as they derive from a ball game, and this must happen from the beginning of their lives."

—

Zoltan Kodaly

"Teach music and singing at school in such a way that it is not a torture but a joy for the pupil; instill a thirst for finer music in him, a thirst which will last for a lifetime."

—

Zoltan Kodaly

"Often a single experience will open the young soul to music for a whole lifetime."

—

Zoltan Kodaly

"Let us take our children seriously! Everything else follows from this…only the best is good enough for a child."

Zoltan Kodaly

"To teach a child an instrument without first giving him preparatory training and without developing singing, reading and dictating to the highest level along with the playing is to build upon sand."

Igor Stravinsky

"My music is best understood by children and animals."

Charles Mingus

"Let my children have music! Let them hear live music."

Jean Ashworth Bartle

"Teaching music to children is the most important thing in life, next to parenting, that a person can do."

Plato

"The music masters familiarize children's minds with rhythms and melodies, thus making them more civilized, more balanced, better adjusted in themselves, and more capable in whatever they say or do, for rhythm and harmony are essential to the whole of life."

P. T. Barnum

"To me, there is no picture so beautiful as smiling, bright-eyed, happy children; no music so sweet as their clear and ringing laughter."

Bette Midler

"All these children who did not have music and art classes at school go out into the world without knowing that there is anything other than what they have. Of course, children do look at TV, but what does it give them?"

Maria Montessori

"There should be music in the child's environment, just as there does exist in the child's environment spoken speech. In the social environment, the child should be considered, and music should be provided."

—

William Arthur Ward

"A mediocre music teacher tells. A good music teacher explains. A superior music teacher demonstrates. A great music teacher inspires."

—

Kurt Masur

"If every school would hire two more music teachers, we would need two fewer police officers."

—

Jill Sobule

"Music teachers can either inspire or make you resent your instrument and parents in the early years."

Ed Droste

"My mother was a music teacher and my grandfather was a professor of music, and there was a lot of singing in the family. It wasn't like trained singing or anything like that, but it was singing."

—

Shakira

"The music teacher thought I sang like a goat. It was kind of devastating. A few months after that, I participated in a music contest and won. I took my little trophy to school and rubbed it in his nose. I said to him, 'What do you say now?'"

—

Elvis Presley

"I don't know anything about music. In my line, you don't have to."

Zach Braff

"As a kid who wasn't into sports, at school I felt almost alienated at times, whereas in the theatre community there was this amazing sense of camaraderie. Early on, we would go to rehearsals with my dad and I was like the mascot for the backstage crew. That was a big part of my childhood, so I dreamed of one day doing a play in London."

―

Robert Jay Lifton

"As a kid, I was fascinated with sports, and I loved sports more than anything else. The first books I read were about sports, like books about Baseball Joe, as one baseball hero was called."

―

David Duchovny

"When I was a kid, I ate sportsbooks up, like "Winners Never Quit" by Phil Pepe. That was like my bible."

My parents taught me I could be anything in the world I wanted to be.
—Joan Jett

Mark Teixeira

"My greatest memories as a kid were playing sports with my dad and watching sports with my dad."

—

Joe DiMaggio

"There is always some kid who may be seeing me for the first time. I owe him my best."

—

Joe DiMaggio

"A ballplayer has to be kept hungry to become a big leaguer. That's why no boy from a rich family has ever made the big leagues."

—

Joe DiMaggio

"If anyone wants to know why three kids in one family made it to the big leagues, they just had to know how we helped each other and how much we practiced back then. We did it every minute we could."

Quotes for Parents

Wayne Gretzky

"I think sports for kids is the greatest thing in the world because it teaches you how to share, about winning and losing and pressure. But I don't think you should force your kid to become a professional athlete."

Michael Keaton

"I played a lot of sports when I was a kid so I get in that ballgame mindset of being really, really respectful, but at the same time saying to yourself, 'Don't back down a single inch, hang with these guys if you can.' If they throw it high and tight you have to stand in there, you can't take yourself out of that moment."

Sugar Ray Leonard

"Boxing's a poor man's sport. We can't afford to play golf or tennis. It is what it is. It's kept so many kids off the street. It kept me off the street."

Sugar Ray Leonard

"I found boxing when I was 14 years old. I went down to the gym because my brother, who used to beat me up all the time, introduced me to boxing. I found boxing to be a sport that I felt safe in because I controlled what was in those four squares."

—

Francine Prose

"I remember, when I was a little kid, I was good at sports, and I could jump off the high board. And then puberty hit, and suddenly I was looking to boys for direction. I remember that as a great loss."

—

Armstrong Williams

"Sports nurtures dreams of achieving self-confidence and masculine striving for the skinny kid watching a boxer dance around the ring with sublime ease."

—

Quotes for Parents

Paul McAllister

"College coaches measure success in championships. High School coaches measure success to titles. Youth coaches measure success in smiles."

—

Tony Hale

"I was a creative kid; I wasn't really into sports, and sports in the South are a pretty big deal. It's like a religion down there. It was tough to find my footing, but thankfully, my parents discovered, through a neighbor, this theater called Young Actors Theater and signed me up for the summer program. It really was a gift. Even if a kid doesn't go into acting or the arts like I did, some kids need that environment to find themselves and find what they love to do. I'm so thankful for that theater; it was a big gift to me."

—

Rafael Nadal

"Since I was a kid, I've wanted to do sports for a living. In the beginning, I played a lot of soccer, but in the end, I chose tennis. I love sports in general ... But tennis is my passion."

Quotes for Parents

Bobby Orr

"I couldn't wait to get on the ice. I couldn't wait to get to practice. As a kid, I couldn't wait to shoot pucks or play in parking lots or play on the river or play on the bay."

Mo Rocca

"I wish I had played team sports. I think every kid should. Teamwork builds character - teaches people about leadership and cooperation."

Patrick Chan

"I tried all kinds of sports when I was a kid, like soccer and tennis and golf, and in fact, started skating to be able to play hockey."

Aaron Tveit

"I didn't grow up a theatre kid, going to theatre camps. I played sports, and that was my main direction. But luckily, I never had to choose between sports and theatre."

—

Hugh Jackman

"One afternoon when I was 9, my dad told me I'd be skipping school the next day. Then we drove 12 hours from Melbourne to Sydney for the Centenary Test, a once-in-a-lifetime commemorative cricket match. It was great fun - especially for a kid who was a massive sports fan."

—

Jack Nicklaus

"You get the kids today into the sport, and then they can't get to the "next level." I mean, come on, that's a bunch of junk."

—

Play is the highest form of research.

— Albert Einstein

Quotes for Parents

Pregnancy, because it all begins, with a big belly

The last section of quotes many will feel should have been first. After all, a child begins with a big belly and before that the messy icky kissy-kissy that so disgusts kids and delights teenagers, as long as it's not mom and dad.

Today wonderful people become wonderful parents without the big belly and all that comes with pregnancy. They adopt, take in foster children or care for a family members child when they are unable to do so.

Then there are parents that fall in love and the kids get taken along the trip to be a larger family.

No matter how you become a parent it's an amazing job and our hats are off to you. This chapter is about the pregnancy and a tad about the bundles of leaking fluids and tiny finger that grow into the annoying teenagers.

Matthew Stout

> EVEN FOR PARENTS OF CHILDREN THAT ARE NOT ON THE SPECTRUM, THERE IS NO SUCH THING AS A NORMAL CHILD.
>
> — VIOLET STEVENS

Carrie Fisher

"Everything grows rounder and wider and weirder, and I sit here in the middle of it all and wonder who in the world you will turn out to be."

—

Tori Spelling

"I'm never as happy as when I'm pregnant. I literally would have 10 babies if I could!"

—

Holly Madison

"Truthfully, being pregnant is changing me as a person. Each day is part of this amazing journey that has completely shifted the focus of my life and made me reevaluate my personal and professional goals."

—

Jessica Simpson

"People always say that pregnant women have a glow. And I say it's because you're sweating to death."

—

Nora Ephron

"If pregnancy were a book, they would cut the last two chapters."

—

Rita Rudner

"Life is tough enough without having someone kick you from the inside."

—

Irena Chalmers

"There are three reasons for breast-feeding: the milk is always at the right temperature; it comes in attractive containers, and the cat can't get it."

—

Laurence Housman

"If nature had arranged that husbands and wives should have children alternatively, there would never be more than three in a family."

—

Elayne Boosler

"People are giving birth underwater now. They say it's less traumatic for the baby because it's underwater. But it's certainly more traumatic for the other people in the pool."

—

E. B. White

"Life is always rich and steady time when you are waiting for something to happen or to hatch."

—

Erma Bombeck

"Never go to your high school reunion pregnant or they will think that is all you have done since you graduated."

—

Brigitte Bardot

"I am not finding pregnancy much of a joy. I am afraid of childbirth, but I am afraid I can't find a way of avoiding it."

—

Sam Levenson

"Somewhere on this globe, every ten seconds, there is a woman giving birth to a child. She must be found and stopped."

—

Al Roker

"In the pregnancy process, I have come to realize how much of the burden is on the female partner. She's got a construction zone going on in her belly."

—

Brooke Burke

"Going into a pregnancy is a really challenging time for a woman, because it's forever changing, both mentally and physically."

—

Crescent Dragonwagon

"All the time we wondered and wondered, who is this person coming/growing/turning/floating/swimming deep, deep inside."

Benjamin Franklin

"A ship under sail and a big-bellied woman, Are the handsomest two things that can be seen common."

Michel Odent

"I usually claim that pregnant women should not read books about pregnancy and birth. Their time is too precious. They should, rather, watch the moon and sing to their baby in the womb."

Phyllis Diller

"By far the most common craving of pregnant women is not to be pregnant."

Jodi Sweetin

"I think as a pregnant woman we're all looking for stuff that makes us all look cute and fashionable and feel sexy when we're pregnant."

Grey DeLisle

"Many thanks for all of the love and good wishes sent our way from my friends out there in cartoon land... the only place where a nine-month pregnant woman can still play a hot goth chick in a belly shirt!"

Sheila Kitzinger

"All that is needed for the majority of labors to go well is a healthy, pregnant woman who has loving support in labor, self-confidence, and attendants with infinite patience."

Ashlee Simpson

"My weight and my pant size are the absolute last thing I'm concerned about. People who talk and judge pregnant women's weight need to get a life!"

Audrey Niffenegger

"My reflection in the mirror shows me pink and puffy. I thought pregnant women were to supposed to glow. I am not glowing."

—

Dave Barry

"Advice to expectant mothers: you must remember that when you are pregnant, you are eating for two. But you must remember that the other one of you is about the size of a golf ball, so let's not go overboard with it. I mean, a lot of pregnant women eat as though the other person they're eating for is Orson Welles."

—

Keri Russell

"People expect all women to react the same to pregnancy. But anyone who's been around pregnant women knows that it's not all cutesy and sweet. You spaz out and you're angry and you have tantrums."

—

Georgia May Jagger

"I always see those jeans with the stretchy front on pregnant women, and they look like the dreamiest thing ever."

—

Chris Mohr

"About 70 percent of pregnant women are deficient in Vitamin D."

—

Desiderius Erasmus

"Heaven grant that the burden you carry may have as easy an exit as it had an entrance."
Prayer To A Pregnant Woman

—

Kourtney Kardashian

"I loved dressing for my pregnant body. A pregnant woman's body is so beautiful. Towards the end, it does get harder, and then it became all about flats and comfortable maxi dresses."

—

Peter Jackson

"A pregnant woman is like a beautiful flowering tree, but take care when it comes time for the harvest that you do not shake or bruise the tree, for in doing so, you may harm both the tree and its fruit."

—

A. Milne

"Sometimes,' said Pooh, 'the smallest things take up the most room in your heart."

—

Martin Farquhar Tupper

"A babe in the house is a well-spring of pleasure, a messenger of peace and love, a resting place for innocence on earth, a link between angels and men."

—

Georges Courteline

"One of the most obvious results of having a baby around the house is to turn two good people into complete idiots who probably wouldn't have been much worse than mere imbeciles without it."

—

"YOU NEVER KNOW HOW MUCH YOUR PARENTS LOVED YOU UNTIL YOU HAVE A CHILD TO LOVE."

— Jennifer Hudson

Eda LeShan

"A new baby is like the beginning of all things - wonder, hope, a dream of possibilities."

—

Vincent Van Gogh

"If one feels the need of something grand, something infinite, something that makes one feel aware of God, one need not go far to find it. I think that I see something deeper, more infinite, more eternal than the ocean in the expression of the eyes of a little baby when it wakes in the morning and coos or laughs because it sees the sun shining on its cradle."

—

Don Herold

"Babies are such a nice way to start people."

—

Virginia Clinton Kelley

"There is nothing like a newborn baby to renew your spirit - and to buttress your resolve to make the world a better place."

Amy Heckerling

"Babies don't need fathers, but mothers do. Someone who is taking care of a baby needs to be taken care of."

T. S. Eliot

"If you desire to drain to the dregs the fullest cup of scorn and hatred that a fellow human being can pour out for you, let a young mother hear you call dear baby 'it'."

Desiderius Erasmus

"Everyone knows that by far the happiest and universally enjoyable age of man is the first. What is there about babies which makes us hug and kiss and fondle them, so that even an enemy would give them help at that age?"

Benjamin Spock

"The more people have studied different methods of bringing up children the more they have come to the conclusion that what good mothers and fathers instinctively feel like doing for their babies is the best after all."

—

Steven Wright

"Babies don't need a vacation, but I still see them at the beach... it pisses me off! I'll go over to a little baby and say 'What are you doing here? You haven't worked a day in your life!'"

—

Eleanor Roosevelt

"The kind of man who thinks that helping with the dishes is beneath him will also think that helping with the baby is beneath him, and then he certainly is not going to be a very successful father."

—

May Sarton

"Don't forget that compared to a grownup person every baby is a genius. Think of the capacity to learn! The freshness, the temperament, the will of a baby a few months old!"

—

Katie Holmes

"I feel very lucky. I have a husband and baby that I adore. I have a career I really love. When I sit back and reflect, it's, like, wow! I am very grateful."

—

Ron L. Hubbard

"Maintain silence in the presence of birth to save both the sanity of the mother and the child and safeguard the home to which they will go."

—

Gail Porter

"I didn't have any problem bonding with Honey, but I was plagued with insecurities about my ability to bring up my baby."

—

Jean Kerr

"Now the thing about having a baby - and I can't be the first person to have noticed this - is that thereafter you have it."

—

Paul Reiser

"Having a baby dragged me, kicking and screaming, from the world of self-absorption."

—

Tris Speaker

"If you put a baseball and other toys in front of a baby, he'll pick up a baseball in preference to the others."

—

Erica Jong

"A baby's a full-time job for three adults. Nobody tells you that when you're pregnant, or you'd probably jump off a bridge. Nobody tells you how all-consuming it is to be a mother-how reading goes out the window and thinking too."

James M. Barrie

"When the first baby laughed for the first time, the laugh broke into a thousand pieces and they all went skipping about, and that was the beginning of fairies."

—

Trista Sutter

"A baby fills a hole in your heart that you didn't know was there."

—

Matthew Broderick

"Having a baby changes the way you view your in-laws. I love it when they come to visit now. They can hold the baby and I can go out."

—

Mark Twain

"A baby is an angel whose wings decrease as his legs increase."

Anne Morrow Lindbergh

"In the sheltered simplicity of the first days after a baby is born, one sees again the magical closed circle, the miraculous sense of two people existing only for each other."

Mark Twain

"Adam and Eve had many advantages, but the principal one was that they escaped teething."

M. Russell Ballard

"The joy in motherhood comes in moments. There will be hard times and frustrating times, but amid the challenges, there are shining moments of joy and satisfaction."

Jayne Mansfield

"Carrying a baby is the most rewarding experience a woman can enjoy."

Steven Wright

"My friend has a baby. I'm recording all the noises he makes so later I can ask him what he meant."

George MacDonald

"Where did you come from, baby dear? Out of the everywhere and into here."

Marilyn Monroe

"I learned to walk as a baby, and I haven't had a lesson since."

Shannon Fife

"Insomnia: A contagious disease often transmitted from babies to parents."

Telly Savalas

"We're all born bald, baby."

—

Lily Aldridge

"I think I'm going to give my baby her first food on Thanksgiving, make her some organic sweet potato. I'm very excited! It's going to be a big day and my husband is in charge of the turkey - he's the chef of the family!"

—

Ray Romano

"When you wake up one day and say, "You know what? I don't think I ever need to sleep or have sex again." Congratulations, you're ready (to have children)."

—

Anne Lamott

"Feeding a baby is like filling a hole with putty - you get it in and then you sort of shave off all the excess around the hole and get it back in like you're spackling."

Anne Lamott

"You fall so deeply in love with your grandbaby. It's so, so, so much easier than being a parent because you really don't have much responsibility. And just when you are at the end of your rope with exhaustion, the parents take the baby away. So, it's the best of both worlds."

Cindy Margolis

"You check the pregnancy test every month, and when it comes up negative it can start to wear on you"

Lizz Winstead

"And home pregnancy tests? They are so last century. Nowadays, I think there's an app that calls your iPhone to warn you that if you finish that third cosmo, you may wind up with a wombmate."

Gabriel "Fluffy" Iglesias

"Walgreens, Rite Aid, CVS, and Wal-Mart have all figured out the evolution of life and they grabbed all the products that are necessary for a life. And they stuck them in one aisle, and they put them in order according to how you mess up... First thing you're going to see: condoms. Next to that: lubricant. Next to that: pregnancy test. Next to that: Pampers. Next to that: formula. And at the end of the aisle, they sell beer."

—

Meg Ryan

"All of motherhood surprised me. It surprised me from the very first second I saw Jack. I'd believed that my pregnancy was a condition. It never computed. And there he was. Everyone made fun of me because I stared at him for months and months, not being able to believe he was real."

—

Natasha Hamilton

"Every four weeks I go up a bra size... it's worth being pregnant just for the breasts."

—

Maggie Scarf

"Pregnancy is getting company inside one's skin."

—

Kate Beckinsale

"When I was pregnant, I had the romantic idea that after the baby was born, I would not only take up reading in earnest again but also write a novel while my daughter slept in her Moses basket. Of course, I barely had time to keep up with my magazines until she started sleeping properly."

—

Neneh Cherry

"When I found out I was pregnant, my mother said, 'Don't separate your life, the life that you're going to make with this child, from the things that you are and what you want to do.'"

—

Heidi Klum

"I always think, look at how people were before they were pregnant. If you were a toned, healthy, energetic person, most likely you will be like that again."

—

Jessica Alba

"I did research when I was pregnant with my first daughter and was horrified by the chemicals in products, even those meant for babies. I would have to go to 50 different places just to get my house and my kid clean."

—

Tamera Mowry

"Finding out I was pregnant was one of the most joyous moments in my life. I will never forget it."

—

Suzanne Vega

"When I was pregnant, I felt filled with life, and I felt really happy. I ate well, and I slept well. I felt much more useful than I'd ever felt before."

—

Dave Lombardo

"We got off the Clash of the Titans tour and I said that my wife and I were working on having a baby and sure enough we found out that she was pregnant. So, I told them nine months in advance that I wasn't going to tour in September so I could witness the birth of my first son."

—

Michael Weatherly

"My wife gets pampered pretty well. She's had me trained since she was pregnant when I started making her oatmeal with fresh berries every morning."

—

Christine Feehan

"Of course, I can do this. I'm pregnant, not brain damaged. My condition doesn't change my personality."

—

Thomas C Haliburton

"A woman has two smiles that an angel might envy, the smile that accepts a lover before words are uttered, and the smile that lights on the firstborn babe, and assures it of a mother's love"

—

Jodi Picoult

"Sometimes when you pick up your child you can feel the map of your own bones beneath your hands, or smell the scent of your skin in the nape of his neck. This is the most extraordinary thing about motherhood – finding a piece of yourself separate and apart, that all the same, you could not live without."

—

Erma Bombeck

"If I had my life to live over, instead of wishing away nine months of pregnancy, I'd have cherished every moment and realized that the wonderment growing inside me was the only chance in life to assist God in a miracle."

—

Judy Ford

"Pregnancy is a process that invites you to surrender to the unseen force behind all life."

—

—

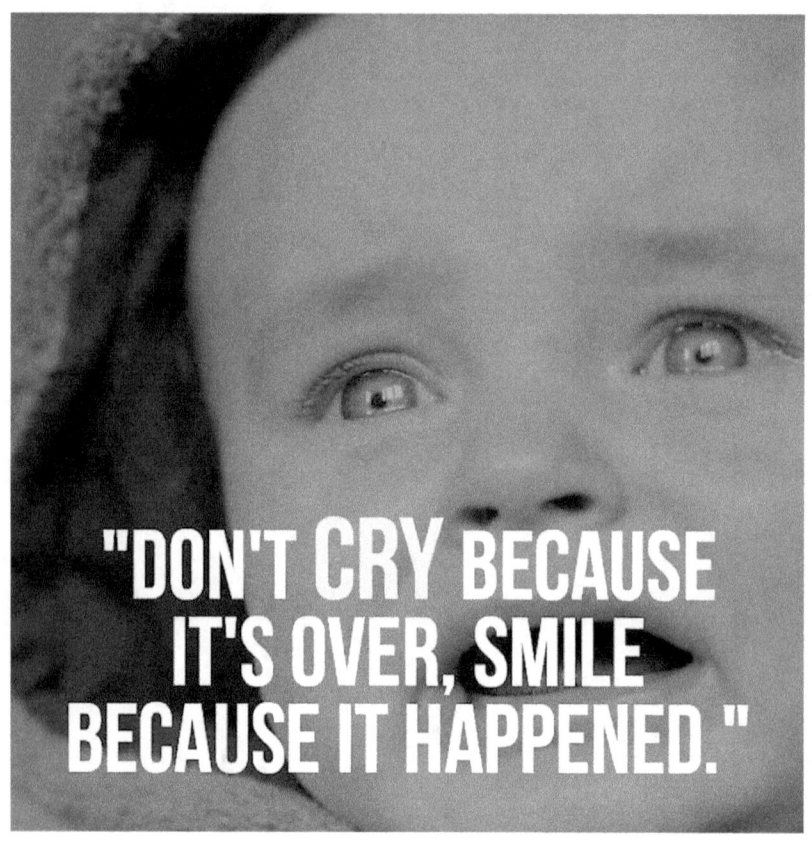

Quotes for Parents

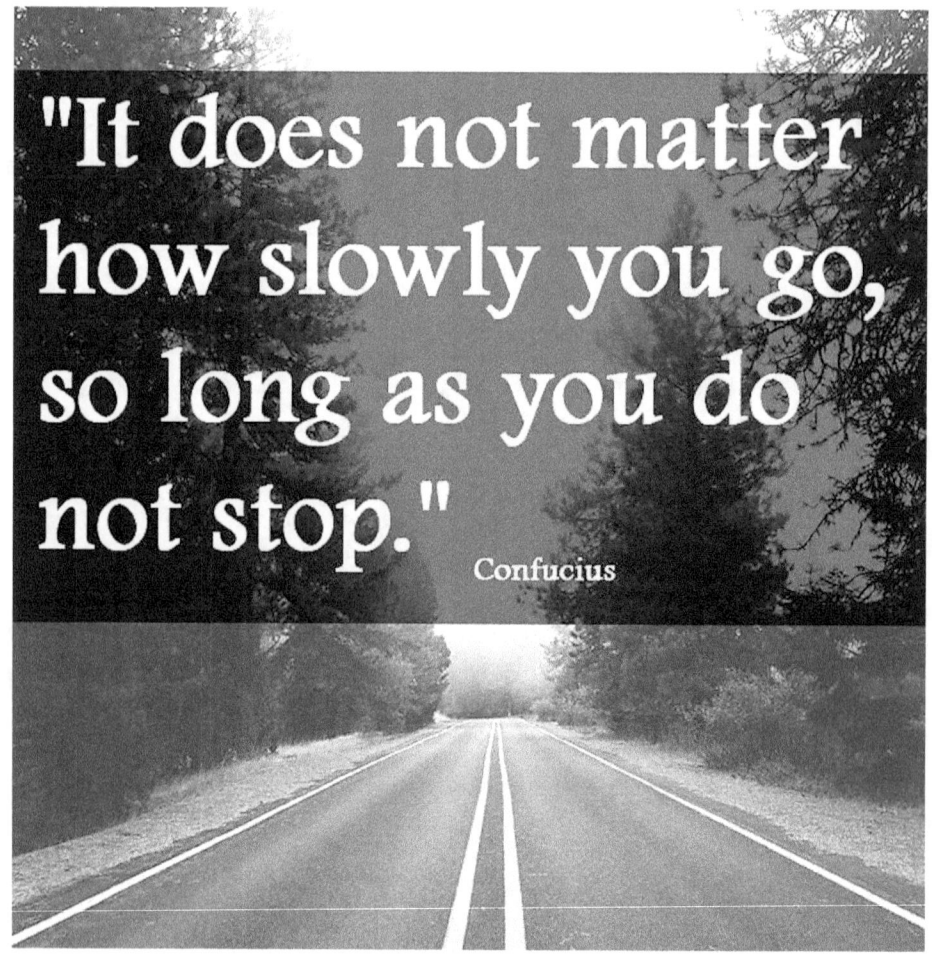

www.ingramcontent.com/pod-product-compliance
Lightning Source LLC
LaVergne TN
LVHW052340080426
835508LV00045B/2862